# DISCOURSE ANALYSIS

*Investigating Processes
of Social Construction*

**NELSON PHILLIPS
CYNTHIA HARDY**

Qualitative Research Methods
Volume 50

Sage Publications
International Educational and Professional Publisher
Thousand Oaks   London   New Delhi

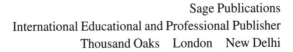

*For information:*

Sage Publications, Inc.
2455 Teller Road
Thousand Oaks, California 91320
E-mail: order@sagepub.com

Sage Publications Ltd.
6 Bonhill Street
London EC2A 4PU
United Kingdom

Sage Publications India Pvt. Ltd.
M-32 Market
Greater Kailash I
New Delhi 110 048 India

Printed in the United States of America

**Library of Congress Cataloging-in-Publication Data**

Phillips, Nelson.
Discourse analysis: investigating processes of social construction /
Nelson Phillips, Cynthia Hardy.
    p. cm.—(Qualitative research methods series; v. 50)
Includes bibliographical references.
ISBN 0-7619-2361-6 (c: alk. paper)
ISBN 0-7619-2362-4 (p: alk. paper)
    1. Discourse analysis—Social aspects. I. Hardy, Cynthia, 1956-II.
Title. III. Qualitative research methods; v. 50.
    P302.84 .P48 2002
    401´.41—dc21
                                        2002002730

This book is printed on acid-free paper.

06  07  08  09  10  9  8  7  6  5  4  3

| | |
|---|---|
| Acquisitions Editor: | Heidi Van Middlesworth |
| Copy Editor: | Elizabeth Budd |
| Production Editor: | Denise Santoyo |
| Typesetter: | Siva Math Setters, Chennai, India |

When citing a university paper, please use the proper form. Remember to cite the Sage University Paper series title and include the paper number. One of the following formats can be adapted (depending on the style manual used):

(1) Phillips, N., & Hardy, C. (2002) *Discourse Analysis: Investigating Processes of Social Construction.* Sage University Papers Series on Qualitative Research Methods, Vol. 50. Thousand Oaks, CA: Sage.

OR

(2) Phillips, N., & Hardy, C. (2002). *Discourse Analysis: Investigating Processes of Social Construction.* (Sage University Papers Series on Qualitative Research Methods, Vol. 50). Thousand Oaks, CA: Sage.

# CONTENTS

# SERIES EDITORS' INTRODUCTION

How do our notions of a "nation," the "individual," or even the "social" come about, solidify, shift, reemerge, and guide our thought and action? How do such taken-for-granted ideas concerning work, family, freedom, and authority become seemingly natural, objective, autonomous features of the world? How do these presuppositions influence, for example, the way we judge refugees as attractive and welcome or disruptive and dangerous? Or more critically, what is a refugee anyway? What constitutes the definitional character of such a label, and when do we apply it to specific people and groups? What are the consequences of our talk (and application)?

These questions (and more) are bedrock dilemmas associated with any investigation of the social world. They are messy matters to say the least, but they cut to the core of social science and raise quite serious empirical, epistemological, and philosophical questions about what is "real." They are subversive questions to be sure. When taken seriously, they undermine our often too confident sense that language and representation are unproblematic. To examine discourse requires an investigator to ask—in highly specified contexts—just how particular ideas, concepts, and perspectives come into being and are sustained. Moreover, it asks what the consequences are of a specified discourse for particular parties (some of whom may not have had much to do with the forming of a set discourse but must nonetheless live with the results).

Nelson Phillips and Cynthia Hardy, in this the 50th volume of the Sage Series on Qualitative Research Methods, provide a crisp, elegant, and quite practical introduction to this growing field. *Discourse Analysis*, as the authors make clear, is more than a simple method of discovery. It rests on a powerful theory detailing and explaining how the social world is understood. The empirical materials of discourse consist of sets of texts and the practices that surround their production, dissemination, and reception. As a domain of study, discourse analysis concerns not only selected texts but the history and context associated with these texts. How such texts can be unpacked and understood as "reality constructors" is the point and purpose of this volume. Both are worthy, timely, and well served.

J. V. M.
P. K. M.
M. L. M.

# PREFACE

What is discourse analysis? How do I do it? These two questions, asked in different ways by a variety of students and colleagues, have led us to write this book. The recent interest in discourse analysis as a method has led to a growing number of books and articles on the topic. However, no book has appeared that provides a concise, straightforward guide to the practice of discourse analysis combined with a discussion of the philosophy that underlies it. We have tried to fill this gap in the literature by providing a concise practical guide for researchers who are interested in understanding and using discourse analysis. The book has been written with a broad and diverse audience in mind: doctoral students who are starting out their careers by embarking on discourse analysis; more seasoned researchers who are turning to discourse analysis to complement other modes of inquiry; experienced discourse analysts who are interested in seeing how other researchers have used this methodology; and finally to academics who want to learn about discourse analysis to understand other authors' work even if they do not intend to use it themselves.

How successful we are in providing a guide that motivates and helps aspiring discourse analysts we leave to our readers to judge. We do know that, from our perspective, it has been a rewarding experience to reflect on how discourse analysts have begun to create their own discourse of organizations through the growing number of conferences, workshops, books, special issues, and articles on the topic and how our own approach has developed within the context of these broader events. Although we find the growth of discourse analysis encouraging, at the same time, we would not want this methodology to become so institutionalized that it loses its highly reflexive nature. As methods become formalized, they run the risk of being reified into a sort of research machine where researchers are reduced to technicians who simply turn a methodological handle and produce "truth." A major advantage of working in a new area is the constant pressure to think about your own role in the research process and to be aware of how you have "made it all up." We have found that the benefits of such regular reflection on the nature of research and the role of the researcher have far outweighed the difficulties of using a relatively undeveloped methodology.

vi

Like all academic work, this book only exists because of the help and creative insights of a number of other people. We are particularly indebted to two friends and colleagues with whom many of the ideas that appear in this book were first developed. Tom Lawrence and Steve Maguire have been our coauthors in a stimulating and productive collaboration that has formed the foundation of our understanding of discourse analysis. Over the course of several research projects, and a number of books and articles, we have learned to apply and explain discourse analysis by working with them. Thanks, guys—we owe you a beer.

We would also like to acknowledge Davide Ravasi, Ian Palmer, and Stewart Clegg, with whom we have written papers we refer to in this book, as well as Susan Ainsworth, André Spicer, David Grant, and Cliff Oswick, who reviewed an early draft of the manuscript. Reading a first draft is never an easy task, and we appreciate the time and effort you all put into reading and commenting on this book. We would also like to thank the editors of Sage's Qualitative Research Methods series, especially John Van Maanen, for their encouragement and insight. On a pragmatic note, this book was written while Nelson Phillips was a Dyason Universitas 21 Visiting Fellow at the University of Melbourne. We would like to acknowledge the University of Melbourne's support, which made the writing of this book possible. Finally, on a more personal note, Nelson would like to thank Deana for her consistent good humor and support despite missed dinners and curtailed vacations. He promises not to write another one for a while. Cynthia would like to thank Jerry for missing that bus—who knows what would have happened to the book otherwise.

# DISCOURSE ANALYSIS

## Investigating Processes of Social Construction

NELSON PHILLIPS
*University of Cambridge*

CYNTHIA HARDY
*University of Melbourne*

## 1. WHAT IS DISCOURSE ANALYSIS?

*Her knowledge of me was so deep, her version so compelling,
that it held together my miscellany of identities. To be sane, we
choose between the diverse warring descriptions of our selves;
I chose hers. I took the name she gave me, and the criticism,
and the love, and I called the discourse me.*

Salman Rushdie, *The Ground Beneath Her Feet* (2000, p. 510)

This book is about discourse. More specifically, it is about the power of
incomplete, ambiguous, and contradictory discourses to produce a social

reality that we experience as solid and real. We understand discourse in the radical, constitutive way of Rushdie's character: The things that make up the social world—including our very identities—appear out of discourse. To put it another way, our talk, and what we are, are one and the same. But we differ from Rushdie's character in that we do not believe individuals always have the luxury of choosing their identity, their truth, and their reality. We think our experience is largely written for us by the multitude of conflicting discourses of which we are a part. This is not to say that we do not strategically draw upon these discourses. We obviously do. But our ability to act strategically is limited by the discourses that accompany our intervention and the complex processes of social construction that precede it. Our view of discourse can be summarized in a sentence: Without discourse, there is no social reality, and without understanding discourse, we cannot understand our reality, our experiences, or ourselves.

Recognizing the profound role of talk and texts in everyday life is only the beginning. This book is also about the process of analyzing discourse and the potential of this methodology for revealing the processes of social construction that constitute social and organizational life. Discourse analysis offers new opportunities for researchers to explore the empirical ramifications of the linguistic turn that has worked its way through the social sciences and humanities in the last 20 years. Whereas other qualitative methods provide well-developed approaches for understanding the social world and the meaning it has for the people in it, discourse analysis goes one step further in embracing a strong social constructivist epistemology (Berger & Luckmann, 1967; Gergen, 1999). It focuses attention on the processes whereby the social world is constructed and maintained. It also includes the academic project itself within its analysis; with its emphasis on reflexivity, discourse analysis aims to remind readers that in using language, producing texts, and drawing on discourses, researchers and the research community are part and parcel of the constructive effects of discourse.

We wrote this book for three reasons. First and foremost, we find discourse analysis to be a compelling theoretical frame for observing social reality. This book represents our attempt to clarify the contribution that discourse analysis can make to the study of individuals, organizations, and societies. Second, we have found discourse analysis to be a useful method in a number of empirical studies and have increasingly adopted it over the last 10 years. We want to encourage other researchers to adopt this approach and believe that a short, simple introduction will help in this regard. Third, we have spent considerable time over the last 10 years struggling with the difficulties of applying discourse analysis to different contexts. By writing this book, we hope to save other researchers from having to go through the same struggles. By providing a general framework for understanding different forms of discourse analysis and applying them to empirical studies of organizational, interorganizational, and societal phenomena, we hope to save other researchers from having to "reinvent the wheel."

## Defining Discourse Analysis

There are many definitions of discourse and discourse analysis in the literature. In fact, in his introduction, van Dijk suggested that the entire 700 pages of the recent two-volume set on discourse (1997a, 1997b) is really an "elaborate answer" to a deceptively simple question: What is discourse? Yet, despite the difficulty of the task, we need some general idea of what we are referring to when we use *discourse analysis* and related terms. We also need to differentiate between discourse analysis and other qualitative methods that explain the meaning of social phenomena. In this section, we present some of the important terms that relate to discourse analysis. We also describe its status as a methodology rather than just a method, that is, an epistemology that explains how we know the social world, as well as a set of methods for studying it. In this way, we differentiate discourse analysis from other qualitative research methods, such as ethnography (Erickson & Stull, 1997; Schwartzman, 1993), ethnomethodology (Coulon, 1995), conversation analysis (Psathas, 1995), and narrative analysis (Czarniawska, 1998; Riessman, 1993).

### Defining Our Terms

Discourse, in general terms, refers to actual practices of talking and writing (Woodilla, 1998). Our use of the term is somewhat more specific: We define a discourse as an interrelated set of texts, and the practices of their production, dissemination, and reception, that brings an object into being (Parker, 1992). For example, the collection of texts of various kinds that make up the discourse of psychiatry brought the idea of an unconscious into existence in the 19th century (Foucault, 1965). In other words, social reality is produced and made real through discourses, and social interactions cannot be fully understood without reference to the discourses that give them meaning. As discourse analysts, then, our task is to explore the relationship between discourse and reality.

Discourses are embodied and enacted in a variety of texts, although they exist beyond the individual texts that compose them. Texts can thus be considered a discursive "unit" and a material manifestation of discourse (Chalaby, 1996). Texts may take a variety of forms, including written texts, spoken words, pictures, symbols, artifacts, and so forth (Grant, Keenoy, & Oswick, 1998).

> Texts are the sites of the emergence of complexes of social meanings, produced in the particular history of the situation of production, that record in partial ways the histories of both the participants in the production of the text and of the institutions that are "invoked" or brought into play, indeed a partial history of the language and the social system, a partiality due to the structurings of relations of power of the participants. (Kress, 1995, p. 122)

Texts are not meaningful individually; it is only through their interconnection with other texts, the different discourses on which they draw, and the nature of their production, dissemination, and consumption that they are made meaningful. Discourse analysis explores how texts are *made* meaningful through these processes and also how they contribute to the constitution of social reality by *making* meaning (Phillips & Brown, 1993).

Discourse analysis is thus interested in ascertaining the constructive effects of discourse through the structured and systematic study of texts (Hardy, 2001). Discursive activity does not occur in a vacuum, however, and discourses do not "possess" meaning. Instead, discourses are shared and social, emanating out of interactions between social groups and the complex societal structures in which the discourse is embedded. Accordingly, if we are to understand discourses and their effects, we must also understand the context in which they arise (Sherzer, 1987; van Dijk, 1997a).

> Discourse is not produced without context and cannot be understood without taking context into consideration. . . . Discourses are always connected to other discourses which were produced earlier, as well as those which are produced synchronically and subsequently. (Fairclough & Wodak, 1997, p. 277)

Our approach to the study of discourse is therefore "three-dimensional" (Fairclough, 1992), in the sense that it connects texts to discourses, locating them in a historical and social context, by which we refer to the particular actors, relationships, and practices that characterize the situation under study.

Consider an example: To understand from a discourse analytic perspective why a particular person is a refugee, we need to explore how discourses such as asylum, immigration, humanitarianism, and sovereignty, among others, serve to make sense of the concept of a refugee. To learn how such discourses have evolved over time, we can study texts such as cartoons, newspaper articles, and international conventions. We must also examine the social context—wars, natural disaster, court decisions, international agreements, the government of the day, political events in other countries—to see how they are brought into play in particular discursive events. This interplay between text, discourse, and context helps us to understand not only how an individual comes to be a refugee, but also how the broader "reality" of refugee policy and refugee determination procedures is constructed and experienced.

In summary, our interest in the relation between discourse and social reality requires us to study individual texts for clues to the nature of the discourse because we can never find discourses in their entirety. We must therefore examine selections of the texts that embody and produce them (Parker, 1992). We cannot simply focus on an individual text, however; rather, we must refer to *bodies* of texts because it is the interrelations between texts, changes in texts, new textual forms, and new systems of distributing texts that constitute a discourse over time. Similarly, we must also make reference to the social context in which the texts are found and the discourses are produced. It is this connection between discourses and the social reality that they constitute that makes discourse analysis a powerful method for studying social phenomena.

## Discourse Analysis as Method and Methodology

The reason discourse analysis tries to include a concern with text, discourse, and context relates to the fact that it represents a methodology—not just a method—that embodies a "strong" social constructivist view of the social world (Gergen, 1999). Discourse analytic approaches share an interest in the constructive effects of language and are a reflexive—as well as an interpretive—style of analysis (Parker & Burman, 1993). In this regard, discourse analysis does not simply comprise a set of techniques for conducting structured, qualitative investigations of texts; it also involves a set of assumptions concerning the constructive effects of language.

> [Discourse analysis] is not only about method; it is also a perspective on the nature of language and its relationship to the central issues of the social sciences. More specifically, we see discourse analysis as a related collection of approaches to discourse, approaches that entail not only practices of data collection and analysis, but also a set of metatheoretical and theoretical assumptions and a body of research claims and studies. (Wood & Kroger, 2000, p. x)

Discourse analysis shares the concern of all qualitative approaches with the meaningfulness of social life (Winch, 1958), but it attempts to provide a more profound interrogation of the precarious status of meaning. Traditional qualitative approaches often assume a social world and then seek to understand the meaning of this world for participants. Discourse analysis, on the other hand, tries to explore how the socially produced ideas and objects that populate the world were created in the first place and how they are maintained and held in place over time. Whereas other qualitative methodologies work to understand or interpret social reality as it exists, discourse analysis endeavors to uncover the way in which it is produced. This is the most important contribution of discourse analysis: It examines how language constructs phenomena, not how it reflects and reveals it. In other words, discourse analysis views discourse as constitutive of the social world—not a route to it—and assumes that the world cannot be known separately from discourse.

Discourse analysis is thus distinguished by its commitment to a strong social constructivist view and in the way it tries to explore the relationships between text, discourse, and context. Although studies vary in the degree to which they combine text and context (as we discuss in Chapter 2), discourse analysis presupposes that it is impossible to strip discourse from its broader context and uses different techniques to analyze texts for clues to the discourses within which they are embedded. In this regard, discourse analysis is different from other forms of qualitative research. For example, approaches such as narrative analysis and conversational analysis typically study text or talk. They take context into account to ascertain meaning, but usually without reference to broader discourses or the accumulated bodies of texts that constitute them. Although interested in how narratives and conversations are constructed, these approaches devote less explicit attention to the construction of a broader social reality. Similarly, ethnographies often aim at uncovering the meaning of a social reality for participants but are less concerned with how that social reality came into existence through the constructive effects of various discourses and associated texts. Ethnomethodology focuses on the generative rules that make social interrelationships possible, but its focus is on the observation of actions rather than on the study of texts. In Box 1.1, we provide an example to show the ways in which quantitative and qualitative researchers might approach a phenomenon and contrast them with how discourse analysts would study it.

**Box 1.1**
**Example: The Analysis of Globalization**

A *quantitative* study of globalization might involve collecting information on the degree to which globalization activities are evident in a particular setting. Researchers might collect statistics on foreign direct investment, the number of strategic alliances with overseas companies, decisions of the World Trade Organization, the use of technology in developing countries, the size and nature of trade flows, or indicators concerning the prevalence of a global pop culture. Such studies would attempt to connect the degree of globalization, as denoted by these quantitative indicators, with particular outcome measures such as profitability, poverty, demographic trends, and so forth. Such research takes the concept of globalization for granted and seeks to ascertain relationships among particular practices and outcomes to draw conclusions about the prevalence or effectiveness of globalization.

*Qualitative* studies of globalization can take a number of forms. For example, an ethnography might involve a researcher living in a small village in a developing country to ascertain the meaning and impact of new Internet connections for villagers; how the presence of multinational companies affects family life; or how global calls for bans on child labor influence economic and social well-being. A researcher could also undertake an ethnographic study of an Indian-based call center, in which he or she observes how employees present themselves—via telephone—to callers from around the world and what this means for the employees of the organization. One could use narrative analysis to uncover the stories that people tell to explain new global practices, using devices such as plot, narrator, and characters to ascertain how they make sense of a new Internet café, an international merger, or the sudden disappearance of an overseas market. One might use conversation analysis to study teenagers in different countries talking among themselves about what MTV means to them and what they consider important about their dress style. One could conduct interviews with key actors in the World Trade Organization or the United Nations to ascertain their views on the North–South

**Box 1.1** *(continued)*

divide and compare their comments with the opinions of officials in governments of southern counties. A researcher's political analysis might use unstructured interviews and participant observation to uncover the politics and cultural dislocation involved in a takeover of a local firm by a U.S. multinational corporation and to highlight any actions—covert or overt—by unions, employees, and community members to resist or influence the changes. Such qualitative studies are all, in different ways, interested in the social and political dynamics associated with globalization practices and in what those practices mean to individuals who are affected by them. These researchers are interested in the meaning, rather than the "facts," of globalization, but they still take the concept of globalization as "given."

*Discourse analysis* is interested in how the concept of globalization came about—why it has a particular meaning today when, 60 years ago, it had none. Researchers might explore how globalization discourse draws from and influences other discourses—such as free trade discourse and liberalism, discourse around new technology, poverty and democracy, and even health and terrorism—and how it is constructed through diverse texts that range from academic articles to CNN newscasts. They might then investigate how this broad discourse of globalization gives meaning and substance to disjointed and contradictory patterns of economic, social, geographic, and cultural activities. At the local level, researchers might explore how the discourse of globalization makes certain practices possible or inevitable—such as the business operations of multinational companies, restrictions on refugees, or trade patterns between countries—and how it empowers and disempowers different identities. They may also investigate how particular actors draw on the globalization discourse to legitimate their positions and actions. In exploring different texts pertaining to globalization and relating them to the broader economic, social, and political context, as well as to more specific practices, discourse analysts are able to draw conclusions that undermine the very notion of globalization, showing how it is neither inevitable nor complete but, in fact, a confluence of discourses, texts, and practices that make up a particular reality.

**Table 1.1**     Diversity in Data and Traditions of Discourse Analysis

| *Examples of Data in Discourse Analysis* | *Examples of Traditions in Discourse Analysis* |
| --- | --- |
| • Interviews | • Conversation analysis |
| • Focus groups | • Foucauldian research |
| • Documents and records | • Critical discourse analysis |
| • Naturally occurring conversations | • Critical linguistics |
| • Political speeches | • Discursive psychology |
| • Newspaper articles | • Bakhtinian research |
| • Cartoons | • Interactional linguistics |
| • Novels | • Ethnography of speaking |

SOURCE: Adapted from Wetherell, M. (2001). Debates in discourse research. In M. Wetherell, S. Taylor, and S. J. Yates (Eds.), *Discourse theory and practice: A reader* (p. 38). Thousand Oaks, CA: Sage.

It is important to note, however, that some traditional qualitative approaches do lend themselves to discourse analysis. For example, conversation analysis and narrative analysis can be used to connect "microevents" to broader discourses as a way to show how narratives and conversations construct social experience (e.g., O'Connor, 1995; Stokoe, 1998; van Dijk, 1993). Similarly, ethnographies have been an important component of discourse analytic studies in showing how discourses are enacted in particular practices (e.g., Covaleski, Dirsmith, Heian, & Sajay, 1998; Fletcher, 1998 Jackall, 1988; Orr, 1996). Content analysis, not in terms of a mechanistic counting but in a more interpretive form, can be used to connect textual content to broader discursive contexts. For example, Ellingson (1995) carried out a content analysis of newspaper articles and editorials by identifying themes and rhetorical strategies and connecting them to the speaker and the audience; Holmes (1998) conducted a content analysis of women's language use by linking it to power and status. Although the philosophy underpinning discourse analysis differentiates it from other forms of analysis, when it comes to actual studies, the boundaries between discourse analysis and other qualitative methods are sometimes blurred. Researchers have consequently employed a range of interpretive techniques—from microanalyses of individual utterances to macroanalyses of a corpus of texts—to undertake discourse analysis and, as Table 1.1 shows, they have borrowed from traditional qualitative methods to do so.

What makes a research technique discursive is not the method itself but the *use* of that method to carry out an interpretive analysis of some form of text with a view to providing an understanding of discourse and its role in constituting social reality. To the extent that they are used within a discourse analytic ontology and epistemology, many qualitative techniques can become discourse methods.

One final characteristic of discourse analysis is also worth noting: Discourse analytic methods are unavoidably reflexive because the strong social constructivist epistemology that forms its foundation applies equally to the work of academic researchers. Academic discourse also constitutes a particular reality, and we are continuously challenged to retain a sensitivity to our role in the constitution of categories and frames that produce a reality of a particular sort (see Marcus, 1994). Whereas other approaches tend to take analytic categories for granted and allocate data to them, discourse analysts are interested in the socially constructed nature of the research categories themselves.

> Thus the task of discourse analysis is not to apply categories to participants' talk, but rather to identify the ways in which participants themselves actively construct and employ categories in their talks. Further, all categorization is provisional; analysis requires constant reflexive attention to the process of categorization of both the participant and the analyst. (Wood & Kroger, 2000, pp. 29–30)

Even grounded theory, although it seeks to generate categories from empirical findings, does not problematize them in the way that discourse analysis does. It accepts the researcher's "reading" of the data (subject to carrying out the necessary research protocols). Discourse analysts, on the other hand, are attuned to the co-construction of the theoretical categories at multiple levels, including researcher, research subject, academic community, and even society, and they attempt to design and present their research in ways that acknowledge these complex relationships (Alvesson & Sköldberg, 2000; Clegg & Hardy, 1996a; Hardy, Phillips, & Clegg, 2001).

The need to link text, context, and discourse, and to incorporate a highly subjective and reflexive use of research methods, poses a major challenge for researchers: How do we cope with all this complexity? We can never study all aspects of discourse, and we inevitably have to select a subset of texts for the purpose of manageability. Nonetheless, as discourse analysts we must still make reference to broader discourses, acknowledge the location of individual texts in larger bodies of texts, and pay some attention to three-dimensionality. We are also faced with the prospects of learning by doing as we employ a particular analytical technique, interpreting meanings as we go along and giving voice to multiple meanings. And, having incorporated all this into our study, we have to explain our work within the confines of the normal avenues and arenas of academic publication. It is this complexity and ambiguity that makes discourse analysis such a challenge—and also one of the reasons why we wrote this book, although by this stage, the reader may be left thinking, why bother with discourse analysis at all?

## Reasons for Using Discourse Analysis

In this section, we discuss some of the reasons for using discourse analysis. Given the plethora of other more established methodologies and the difficulties noted above in doing discourse analysis, why should anyone consider using this methodology for his or her empirical research? The reasons *not* to adopt a discourse analytic approach are obvious. First, any new method requires substantial investments of time and energy to master. Discourse analysis is certainly no exception to this rule, especially with the relative shortage of methodological writings and established exemplars to guide newcomers to the field. Second, and even more important, by definition new methods are not institutionalized. Researchers therefore face substantial barriers as they attempt to publish or present work that their colleagues find unfamiliar and that can be difficult to relate to existing work in the field. Researchers who adopt the method face additional risks when their work is evaluated for tenure or promotion because the relative rarity of discourse analytic studies makes their evaluation difficult, and unfamiliar reviewers may not appreciate their value. Third, discourse analysis is a labor-intensive and time-consuming method of analysis. Given the ever-ticking tenure clock and pervasive "publish or perish" culture in academia, there are easier and quicker alternatives for carrying out research.

Despite these problems, we believe that there are many good reasons why discourse analysis has an important role to play in the future of social science. These reasons outweigh the disadvantages of adopting a new and relatively unproven research method and, at a personal level, they have convinced us to use discourse analysis in our own research and led us to write this book to assist others who might want to use the method.

In the remainder of this section, we outline five reasons why researchers should consider using discourse analysis. Some of these reasons are specific to discourse analysis and theory itself, whereas others reflect the changing nature of our particular field of study—organization and management theory. The changing nature of the "organization" has resulted in a growing need to find new ways of studying old topics, as well as effective approaches to studying new topics. At this point, it is worth adding a small disclaimer. Although we have written this book to be as general as possible, and although we feel that the problems and solutions we discuss relate to a number of disciplines, many of our examples are organizational in nature. Yet insofar as organizational studies involves the study of individuals and societies, as well as organizations, the motivation behind the use of discourse analysis in our field is not dissimilar to the reasons driving discourse analysis in other fields.

## The "Linguistic Turn"

Over the last 30 years, a revolution of sorts has swept across the humanities and social sciences. Beginning with the work of linguistic philosophers such as Wittgenstein (1967) and Winch (1958), the idea that language is much more than a simple reflection of reality—that, in fact, it is *constitutive* of social reality—has become commonly accepted. This early work heavily influenced sociologists such as Berger and Luckmann (1967) and anthropologists such as Geertz (1973), whose work formed the foundation of a constructionist view of social phenomena. This view has permeated the social sciences and become well accepted as many disciplines are, in Gergen's (1999, p. 16) terms, "pulsing toward the postmodern" and wrestling with crises of representation and legitimation (Denzin & Lincoln, 1994; Rosenau, 1992).

The recognition of the constructive role of language problematizes the very nature of research as the objectivity, neutrality, and independence of the researcher are called into question, as the nature of what passes for truth and knowledge is scrutinized, and as the question of how things work is replaced by questions about what things *mean* (Winch, 1958). The social sciences are not only about counting—defining and measuring variables and the relationships between them—they are also about interpreting what social relationships signify, to which a long history of qualitative research bears witness. With the linguistic turn, however, the demands of interpretative research are multiplied. As researchers, we are no longer interested simply in what the social world means to the subjects who populate it; we are interested in how and why the social world comes to have the meanings that it does. We are also interested in how we, as researchers, are implicated in that process (Clegg & Hardy, 1996a; Hardy et al., 2001). Discourse analysis, as one method for studying these more reflexive processes of social construction, is therefore attracting increasing attention (Alvesson & Kärreman, 2000a).

As the linguistic turn has swept through disciplines, researchers have turned to discourse analysis to study its implications for empirical research. Although somewhat late in adopting this view compared with the humanities and other areas of social science, researchers in organization and management theory are also beginning to see language as increasingly important (Alvesson & Kärreman, 2000a).[1] The idea that organizations are socially constructed and exist primarily in language (broadly defined) is becoming widely accepted. As a result, researchers are increasingly open to and interested in finding new ways to examine these processes. Discourse analysis provides such a methodology because it is grounded in an explicitly constructionist epistemology that sees language as constitutive and constructive rather than reflective and representative (Wood & Kroger, 2000).

## New and Reconceptualized Topics of Study

Broader changes in society have led to the emergence of new topics for study, which has reinforced the role of discourse analysis as a viable and useful research methodology. For example, the natural environment, globalization, and cultural studies have, relatively recently, captured the interest of researchers in a number of disciplines who have made effective use of discourse analysis. Within the narrower confines of organization and management theory, the study of emotion (e.g., Fineman, 1996; Mumby & Putnam, 1992) is one example of a relatively new area in which discursive approaches have been applied to great effect. New topics of study raise new challenges for researchers by creating new categories and drawing our attention to how boundaries are constructed and held in place. Traditional qualitative approaches may provide insight into the nature of these categories, whereas quantitative research often allows generalizable claims to be made about the relations between categories but neither helps us to understand how these categories came to be nor what holds them in place. In fact, traditional methodologies often reify categories, making them seem natural and enduring. Discourse analysis, on the other hand, provides a way of analyzing the dynamics of social construction that produce these categories and hold the boundaries around them in place.

Other subjects have been reconceptualized by researchers and now require completely different approaches from those used in previous work. For example, identity has long been a subject of study in a number of disciplines, but primarily from an orientation in which researchers attempt to reveal or understand an individual's "true" or essential identity (see Nkomo & Cox, 1996). More recently, discursive approaches are gaining ground in such disciplines as psychology (e.g., Condor & Antaki, 1997; Potter & Wetherell, 1987), gender studies (e.g., Tannen, 1994), organization and management theory (e.g., Calás & Smircich, 1991; Mumby & Stohl, 1991; Wilson, 1996), and social movement theory (e.g., Gamson, 1995) because of the insights provided by an understanding of how identities are constructed on a continuous, interactive, discursive basis.

## The Revitalization of Critical Management Studies

An important reason for the growing appeal of discourse analysis in organization and management theory derives from the renewed interest in critical management studies. Critiques of managerialism have a long-standing tradition in organization and management theory as a result of early Marxist traditions and more radical readings of Weber (Hardy & Clegg, 1996). They appear in a variety of theoretical streams such as labor process theory (e.g., Braverman, 1974; Burawoy, 1979; Edwards, 1979), work on power (e.g., Benton 1981; Clegg, 1975; Hardy, 1985; Lukes, 1974), and studies of culture and ideology (e.g., Smircich, 1983; Weiss and Miller, 1987; Willmott, 1993), to name but a few. The advent of postmodernism in organization and management theory initially challenged this line of thinking (e.g., Burrell, 1988; Cooper & Burrell, 1988). Over time, however, the integration of postmodern and poststructuralist insights has reinvigorated critical management studies and attracted a number of researchers to what is a revitalized agenda in critical management studies (Alvesson & Deetz, 2000; Alvesson & Willmott, 1992a, 1992b; Fournier & Grey, 2000).[2]

Much of the renewed research attention has focused on the intersection between critical and postmodern theory (Alvesson & Deetz, 1996; Mumby, 1992) and, specifically, on the connection between power and meaning—the way in which knowledge is bound up in the dynamics of power (e.g., Knights & Morgan, 1991). Building particularly on the work of

Foucault, researchers have become interested in how processes of social construction lead to a social reality that is taken for granted and that advantages some participants at the expense of others (e.g., Clegg, 1989). At the same time, researchers have sought to examine these political dynamics without falling into the critical trap of "standing outside" the power relations they are studying (Hardy & Clegg, 1996). These new challenges facing critical management studies have created a need for new methods that expose the dynamics on which power distributions in organizations—and in research—depend.

This new and renewed concern with power has not only been confined to organization and management theory. Researchers in areas such as social movement theory, communications, psychology, and gender studies are also increasingly attuned to the dynamics of power. As a result, there are significant opportunities for the application of such methods as critical discourse analysis and critical linguistic analysis (Fairclough, 1992, 1995; Mumby, 2000; Mumby & Stohl, 1991; Parker, 1992) to a variety of settings, in addition to those related to organizations.

## The Development of Postbureaucratic Organizational Forms

Another reason specific to the increased use of discourse analysis in organization and management theory is the changing nature of organizational and management practice over the last few decades. In reflecting on the last 30 years of organization and management theory, Clegg and Hardy (1996b, p. 2) noted that in the 1960s, "hierarchies were the norm, personal computers had not been invented, and the only mode of instantaneous communication was the telephone. The new technologies that were to challenge radically accepted organization designs seemed unthinkable." Today, we witness an array of new organizational forms; the widespread acceptance of new information technologies; the increasing globalization of business, trade, and culture, as well as resistance to it; and the increasing importance of knowledge- and symbol-intensive firms.

These changes in practice have led to a growing need to study the more ephemeral aspects of organizations. It is increasingly difficult to study organizations as if they were solid, fixed material objects when we are aware of their fluid and contradictory dynamics. As a result, we search for the stories, narratives, and symbols—the discourses—that hold together these contradictory flows and make them "real" for us (Chia, 2000). Discourse analysis provides a powerful way to study these slippery, ephemeral phenomena and, as such, is vital if we are to inform and be informed by organizational and management practice.

## The Limits of Traditional Methods and Theories

The final reason we believe that discourse analysis is important grows out of the increasing calls for pluralism that can be heard across the social sciences (e.g., Kaghan & Phillips, 1998). The idea of "one best method" has been challenged more and more frequently; in fact, it has largely been replaced by the idea that research is best served by a plurality of methods and theories (Clegg & Hardy, 1996b). Many researchers have begun to find traditional approaches to research too limiting and repetitive. Rather than using the same method to study the same phenomenon more intensively, the use of a very different method can provide far more insight (Alvesson & Deetz, 2000). Using a nontraditional method provides a way to see things that have been obscured by the repeated application of traditional methods— all ways of seeing are also ways of *not* seeing. Using a discursive approach can allow researchers to build on and complement other bodies of theoretical work by introducing new ideas, new concepts, and new challenges. There is also the fact that it can be more interesting to use less traditional methods to study the world of organizations. They are, by definition, less institutionalized, which allows researchers to use more creativity in their application and more innovation in their interpretation.

In summary, we see discourse analysis as an important contribution to increasing plurality in research, a way to incorporate the linguistic turn and to study new phenomena and practices, as well as to reinvigorate agendas of critical theory. It may pose problems, and old certainties may well disappear but, as Clegg and Hardy (1996b, p. 8) pointed out, "It is in the struggle between different approaches that we learn, and from the diversity and ambiguity of meaning; not through the recitation of a presumed uniformity, consensus, and unity, given in a way that requires unquestioning acceptance."

## What Lies Ahead

This book sets out to help aspiring discourse analysts in four ways. First, we provide a coherent framework for understanding the different forms of discourse analysis that currently appear in the literature. Second, we present a wide range of empirical studies that have been conducted across a range of literatures and show some of the different ways in which discourse analysis can be used. Third, we have used the writing of this book to reflect in some depth on our own work and identify a number of challenges that researchers face as they adopt this method. Finally, we hope to offer some suggestions, based on our own experiences, of how to tackle these challenges.

The remainder of this book is organized in the following way. In Chapter 2, we provide a framework for understanding the different forms of discourse analysis that currently appear in the literature in a variety of disciplines. We begin by focusing on the theoretical assumptions underlying different approaches to discourse analysis and then discuss some of the range of empirical topics that have been explored using discourse analysis. Our intention in Chapter 2 is to provide the reader with a frame for understanding approaches to discourse and an appreciation of the range of potential topics that can be studied using discourse analysis. In Chapter 3, we introduce the reader to our own work in this area. We outline a number of studies we have conducted and explain the types of choices we made in terms of data, data analysis, and general theoretical orientation. We also discuss the contributions that discourse analysis made to our understanding of the phenomena that we studied. In Chapter 4, we explore the question of how to do discourse analysis. Drawing on our experience in carrying out the research program outlined in preceding chapters, we identify some of the key challenges facing researchers embarking on a research project and discuss some of the ways in which they might be addressed. In our final chapter, we sum up our current thoughts on discourse analysis as a field and point to some of the major hurdles that we still need to clear.

## Notes

1. The degree to which social constructivism is accepted in organization and management theory varies geographically. In Europe, few researchers would have difficulty with the basic premises of social constructivism. In North America, it is less accepted, although this is changing rapidly.

2. For example, critical management studies has been established as an integral part of the preconference professional development workshops at the Academy of Management in the United States, and plans exist to apply for interest group status. In the United Kingdom, the first critical management studies conference was held in 1999.

# 2. THE VARIETY OF DISCOURSE ANALYSIS

The definition of discourse analysis presented in the previous chapter was purposefully broad and inclusive. We chose this definition to encompass as many as possible of the different approaches that are referred to as discourse analysis across the social science literature. Our intention was to point to the common ground that makes them all forms of discourse analysis and to distinguish discourse analysis from other forms of social inquiry. In this chapter, we take the opposite tack and focus on the differences among various forms of discourse analysis in terms of their underlying theoretical assumptions and the empirical focus of the research.[1] In this way, we hope to help readers make sense of what is a complex, diverse, and growing field of study.

We begin with an examination of the different theoretical assumptions that underpin empirical work in discourse analysis and that produce quite different styles of research. We present a framework that categorizes these differences according to two key dimensions: the degree to which the emphasis is on individual texts or on the surrounding context and the degree to which the research focuses on power and ideology as opposed to processes of social construction. This framework provides a tool for understanding the diversity of theoretical approaches and for sensitizing researchers to the important epistemological and methodological characteristics of different styles of discourse analysis. As we will show in Chapter 4, understanding the underlying assumptions of different research approaches is important if researchers are to plan and conduct their empirical work successfully.

In the latter part of the chapter, we examine some of the empirical applications that appear in the literature. We feel that more empirical work is needed to complement the theoretical developments that have been made in this area and to use discourse analysis to derive greater insight into a variety of social phenomena. To accomplish this goal, we can build on the existing empirical studies that have been carried out using discourse analysis. By reviewing some of these studies (the coverage here is meant to be illustrative not exhaustive), we can draw attention to the potential of discourse analysis to explore a range of subjects. In addition, we use particular studies as exemplars of particular research orientations that readers may care to consult as models for their own work.

## Theoretical Perspectives in Discourse Analysis

There are many approaches that comprise discourse analysis, and one challenge, particular for newcomers to the field, is to make sense of this diversity. In analyzing a series of empirical studies of discourse analysis, Phillips and Ravasi (1998) found that they could be categorized along two key theoretical dimensions. The first dimension concerns the relative importance of text versus context in the research. The second dimension concerns the degree to which power dynamics form the focus of the research—more critical studies—versus studies that focus more closely on the processes of social construction that constitute social reality—more constructivist studies. Figure 2.1 combines these two dimensions, which are described in more detail below, to identify four main perspectives in discourse analysis.

The vertical axis in Figure 2.1 shows the continuum between *text* and *context*. This continuum may seem surprising given our discussion in the last chapter emphasizing the importance of seeing discourse as being constituted by multiple texts in a particular social and historical context. Demands for three-dimensional research suggest that researchers should include text *and* context in their studies and consider discourse "as a constitutive part of its local and global, social and cultural contexts" (Fairclough, 1995, p. 29). Although this represents an important theoretical ideal, conducting empirical research is another matter as researchers are forced to make choices about the data they select—no researcher can study everything. Whereas the local context of the texts being studied is always relevant (Wetherell, 2001, p. 387), the broader social context can be more or less included depending on the interests and motivations of the researcher. Drawing on the work of Schegloff (1992), Wetherell (2001, p. 388) made a useful distinction between distal and proximate contexts. The distal context "includes things like social class, the ethnic composition of the participants, the institutions or sites where discourse occurs, and the ecological, regional, and cultural settings." The proximate context, on the other hand, refers to the immediate features of the interaction including "the sort of occasion or genre of interaction the participants take an episode to be (e.g., a consultation, an interrogation, a family meal-time), the sequences of talk in which particular events occur and the capacities in which people speak (as initiator or instructor or respondent)" (Wetherell, 2001, p. 338). Whereas the proximate context is always incorporated

20

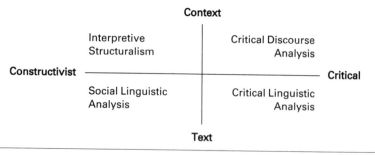

**Figure 2.1**     Different Approaches to Discourse Analysis

in one way or another, the distal context can be more or less included in the analysis depending on practicality and theoretical orientation. Consequently, empirical studies tend to focus more closely on either the broad social context or on a particular piece of text (Alvesson & Kärreman, 2000b; Burman & Parker, 1993; Keenoy, Oswick, & Grant, 1997). Some studies will focus on the microanalysis of particular texts; others will conduct a broader sweep of the discursive elements of particular contexts; and, because this is a continuum not a dichotomy, some studies combine elements of both.

The horizontal axis of Figure 2.1 reflects the choice between *constructivist* approaches that produce fine-grained explorations of the way in which a particular social reality has been constructed, and *critical* approaches, which focus more explicitly on the dynamics of power, knowledge, and ideology that surround discursive processes. Once again, this is a matter of degree because good constructivist studies are sensitive to power, whereas critical studies include a concern for the processes of social construction that underlie the phenomenon of interest. The important question is to what degree do studies focus directly on the dynamics of power—"the relation of language to power and privilege" (Riggins, 1997, p. 2)—as opposed to focusing more directly on the processes of social construction that constitute social reality.

Critical studies are relatively common in discourse analysis. In part, this is due to the influence of Foucault's work, which has led to a body of research on the disciplinary effects of discourse and the relationship between power and knowledge. In addition, the role of discourse theory in reinvigorating critical research agendas, as discussed in Chapter 1, has also led to the development of critically informed empirical work. Critical studies encompass quite different orientations. Foucauldian-informed work often focuses on unmasking the privileges inherent in particular discourses and emphasizes its constraining effects, often leading to studies of how grand or "mega" discourses shape social reality and constrain actors (Alvesson & Kärreman, 2000b). Some researchers reject the notion that there is nothing beyond discourse and, instead, have tried to reassert the idea of a social structure that can empower, as well as disempower, particular actors (e.g., Morgan & Sturdy, 2000). Other researchers have focused more explicitly on the ability of actors to use discourse as a resource to bring about certain outcomes (e.g., Hardy, Palmer, & Phillips, 2000; Jackson, 2000; Phillips & Hardy, 1997).

Not all empirical work is so directly interested in power, however, and many studies explore the constructive effects of discourse without explicitly focusing on the political dynamics. Important bodies of work in disciplines such as sociology (e.g., Gergen, 1991) or psychology (e.g., Harré, 1995; Parker, 1992; Potter & Wetherell, 1987) have led to empirical work that is more interested in developing an understanding of constructive processes than power and politics per se. Rather than exploring who benefits or is disadvantaged by a socially constructed "reality," these researchers are more interested in understanding the way in which discourses ensure that certain phenomena are created, reified, and taken for granted and come to constitute that "reality" (e.g., Dunford & Jones, 2000; Hirsch, 1986).

By combining these two axes, we can identify four major perspectives that are adopted in empirical studies[2]: social linguistic analysis, interpretive structuralism, critical discourse analysis, and critical linguistic analysis (Phillips & Ravasi, 1998). It is important to keep in mind that the dimensions of this framework are continua, not simple categories or dichotomies. The endpoints of the axis of the framework represent ideal types in the Weberian sense: Not all research will necessarily fall neatly into a particular category. However, these four categories do allow us to identify quite different styles of empirical research, which not only helps to orient readers in understanding the literature but which, as we discuss in Chapter 4, is useful for planning research studies. In the remainder of the section, we consider the four perspectives in more detail and discuss an example of empirical work that conforms to each.

## Social Linguistic Analysis

Social linguistic analysis is constructivist and text-based. Much of this work examines specific examples of text and talk such as recordings of conversations (e.g., Kleiner, 1998; Mauws, 2000; Stokoe, 1998), interviews (e.g., Dunford & Jones, 2000; Gill, 1993a, 1993b; van Dijk, 1993), participant observation (Hardy, Lawrence, & Phillips, 1998), focus groups (Beech, 2000), and stories (e.g. Witten, 1993). Researchers focus on individual texts, broadly defined, relating them only marginally to the distal context in which they occur or exploring the power dynamics in which they are implicated. The goal of this work is to undertake a close reading of the text to provide insight into its organization and construction, and also to understand how texts work to organize and construct other phenomena. Common approaches to social linguistic analysis include literary analysis (e.g., O'Connor, 1995), rhetorical analysis (e.g., Mauws, 2000), and the micro discourse analysis commonly carried out in social psychology (e.g., Potter & Wetherell, 1987).

Mauws (2000) provided an example of social linguistic research. Mauws adopted a discourse analytic approach to explore the construction of decisions by a panel of experts as they judged proposals made to Manitoba Film & Sound Development Corporation by musicians seeking financial assistance in commercializing their music. He chose to use discourse analysis to understand the way in which decisions about the potential of a particular individual or band were made. Rather than studying why these experts made the decisions they did, Mauws was interested in the way in which they discursively constructed their decisions. He did not study what was going on in the heads of jury members as they chose between proposals, why they liked one proposal more than another, or even why one proposal was "better" than another. Instead, he focused on the decision as an organizational artifact that was discursively constructed. In this way, his research differentiated between the act of choosing and the process of decision making. And, as part of the decision-making process, he was interested in the rhetorical strategies that were available to the jury members and the "conditions of possibility" (Foucault, 1972) that were present.

The procedures associated with the funding scheme required the group of experts to meet as a jury and render a unanimous verdict. It was this requirement that turned the act of making an individual aesthetic judgment into the discursive act of constructing a decision and made the process appropriate for discursive analysis. The data in this case were a set of transcriptions of jury deliberations. Two meetings each of two juries—one pop music jury and one country music—were recorded in their entirety, transcribed, entered into Atlas.ti,[3] and coded for the rhetorical strategies drawn upon by the juries. The coding began with three broad categories drawn from the existing literature: conformance to genre, imitation, and reputation. A fourth category, innovation, was also discovered in the analysis.

The analysis showed important differences between the pop jury and the country jury, which used these rhetorical strategies in different ways. Mauws (2000, p. 241) noted that "a full repertoire of discursive practices is not available at all times to all those who are speaking; in contrast, it is the context in which people are speaking that predisposes them to use some resources while neglecting others." Although acknowledging that the context—in this case, the difference in the constructions of country and pop music—may influence strategies, it played a background role in Mauws's analysis. His focus was on identifying and understanding the discursive moves—the rhetorical strategies—of judges to construct decisions about what constitutes art in popular and country music. Studies of this kind, which focus on the constructive aspects of texts, help us to understand not only the discursive microdynamics of individual decisions but also the discursive foundations of the social reality in which those decisions are located. They are useful in understanding how social phenomena— decisions, organizations, identities—are produced by specific discursive actions and events on the part of particular actors.

## Interpretive Structuralism

Interpretive structuralism focuses on the analysis of the social context and the discourse that supports it. Some studies focus on the discursive production of organizational or societal contexts. For example, O'Connor (2000) studied organizational change in a high-technology research organization through an examination of the narratives used by managers to construct the change as real and necessary. Heracleous and Barrett (2001) studied organizational change in the context of the London Insurance Market using an interpretive structural approach. Other researchers have focused on the broader, institutional context and its evolution through time. Wodak (1991, 1996), for example, studied the constitution of anti-Jewish prejudice in contemporary Austria based on studies of the reporting of particular events in the Austrian press. Ellingson (1995) explored the conflict between abolitionists and antiabolitionists in antebellum Cincinnati to understand how discourse makes action possible and legitimate based on a study of newspaper articles of the time, as well as other archival material. Although texts may provide some of the data, the description of the context often relies on interviews or archival materials to provide accounts of insiders' interpretations of the context. Even when texts are collected and analyzed, they may be more important as background material because these studies aim at understanding context and on studying data that provide insight into the "bigger picture," rather than a microanalysis of individual texts. As with social linguistic analysis, they are primarily constructivist— concerned with the way in which broader discursive contexts come into being and the possibilities to which they give rise, but without a direct concern with power.

An example of an interpretive structural approach to discourse analysis is Hirsch's (1986) study of hostile takeovers. To understand the changes, from negative to positive, in the social construction of takeovers over time, Hirsch began by collecting data from three major sources. These included articles on takeovers in the *Wall Street Journal, Fortune,* and *Business Week* over a 20-year time period; transcripts of congressional reports and hearings and other publications concerning takeovers; and "candid discussions" with 60 executives involved in takeover activities. These texts provided evidence of the development of the discursive activity around takeovers at a broad societal level; the interviews helped to show how the interpretive frames of the managers were shaped by the broader context. Hirsch retraces the history of the construction of hostile takeovers from its early controversial appearance in the mid-1960s to its progressive spread and establishment as an acceptable, and indeed beneficial, practice in the business community. The reconstruction of historical events was followed by an analysis of various texts to investigate the public linguistic framing of takeover activities, which identified a series of recurring metaphors, ranging from the common "white knight" and "corporate raiders" to the more unusual "sex without marriage," "summer soldiers," and "hired guns." Hirsch also observed how the events associated with a hostile takeover were usually represented in terms of scripts drawn from popular culture. Players were "assigned parts, with each instance coded into the appropriate popular genre, utilizing terminology evocative of the violence, adventure, sex, and conflict found in dramas" (Hirsch, p. 815). These terms were then grouped into genre clusters, associated with settings such as the Western, the love affair, marriage, warfare, mystery and piracy, which varied in the degree of "friendliness" between the parties.

Even though Hirsch did not explicitly refer to his study in such terms, his underlying assumptions about the connections between linguistic framing and social practice allow us to consider his work as a pioneering example of interpretive structural discourse analysis. His findings reveal a number of phases in the discursive construction of takeovers over time to produce an increasingly acceptable, natural, and routine practice. In the earlier period, the linguistic framing of takeovers presented it as an external threat for corporate executives with negative epithets such as "pariah," "pirates," and "raiders." Over time, linguistic frames changed, reflecting as well as driving greater acceptance, until takeovers came to be considered as normal practice—"contests" rather than "conflicts" that were carried out according to the institutionalized normative framework manifested in the "rules of the game" and "good sportsmanship." This analysis of a broad collection of texts over 20 years showed the development of a social discourse that influenced the way members of the business community made sense of, and consequently accepted as legitimate, the emerging practice of takeovers. Interpretive structuralist approaches are thus helpful in understanding macrochanges in broad discourses over periods of time.

## Critical Discourse Analysis

Critical discourse analysis focuses on the role of discursive activity in constituting and sustaining unequal power relations (Fairclough & Wodak, 1997). Critical discourse analysis "should describe and explain how power abuse is enacted, reproduced or legitimated by the talk and text of dominant groups and institutions" (van Dijk, 1996, p. 84). Researchers attempt to analyze "dialogical struggle (or struggles) as reflected in the privileging of a particular discourse and the marginalization of others" (Keenoy et al., 1997, p. 150; Mumby & Stohl, 1991). Drawing particularly on the work of Fairclough, this perspective focuses on how discursive activity structures the social space within which actors act, through the constitution of concepts, objects, and subject positions. Critical discourse analysis focuses on the distal context—how it privileges some actors at the expense of others and how broad changes in the discourse result in different constellations of advantage and disadvantage, particularly within the Foucauldian tradition. See, for example, Knights and Morgan's (1991) study of the development and effects of the discourse of strategy. Other studies using critical discourse analysis adopt a more explicit analysis of how political strategies are shaped by and help to shape this context. For example, Phillips and Hardy's (1997) study of refugee systems showed how certain groups in the refugee system had the right to speak whereas others were silenced and how different groups attempted to draw on discourses that gave them greater rights to speak. Wetherell and Potter (1992) used critical discourse analysis to understand racist discourse in New Zealand and how it functioned to legitimate and explain the political, economic, and social context. Lutz and Collins (1993) also adopted a critical discourse perspective when they studied the role of *National Geographic* in shaping American understandings of non-Western cultures in the United States.

An example of this perspective is Covaleski et al.'s (1998) study of the role of traditional management practices as techniques of social control in professional organizations. The authors were interested in the exercise of, and resistance to, control in the Big Six public accounting firms. The initial purpose was to investigate the involvement of accounting practices and managerial techniques, such as management by objectives (MBO) and mentoring, in the social construction of reality. The authors used an ethnographic field study and drew on Foucault's work to inform data collection and analysis, which allowed them to focus on how disciplinary techniques constituted the identities of one firm's partners and how those identities were resisted.

Data collection was based on 180 in-depth interviews with individuals in different ranks and positions over a period of 15 years. The interviews were aimed at exploring individuals' "lived experience" and "everyday actions and events as they pertained to the exercise of the control and social processes that enabled them to understand and survive in their work environment" (Covaleski et al., 1998, p. 306). Interviews were supplemented by direct observation, archival material, and newspaper coverage of key events in the company. The analysis of these data provided a "thick description" (Geertz, 1973) of the social practices associated with the application of disciplinary techniques, individuals' reactions in terms of compliance or resistance, and implications for the constitution of identity. A broad description of managerial practices and the researchers' interpretation of their discursive function in light of the conceptual framework was presented. Original stories were reported to show that accounts represented people's "interpretations of their own experience" (Covaleski et al., p. 308), providing the "raw material" from which researchers developed their own "provisional" interpretation of the attempt to promote normalization by means of disciplinary techniques such as quantitative measurements.

The use of this approach helped the authors to go beyond the traditional interpretation of control in professional organizations as either residing in bureaucratic practices and procedures or in the internalized norms of a profession. The analysis of discursive practices offered an alternative explanation, according to which control is exercised through technologies—managerial programs—that influence behavior through the constitution of the identity of individuals as manageable and self-serving subjects. Studies conforming to this perspective are thus helpful in revealing the way in which discursive activities help to construct institutions in which power is embedded through the way in which taken-for-granted understandings serve to privilege some actors and disadvantage others. It can also provide insight into the discursive work undertaken by actors in influencing these processes.

## Critical Linguistic Analysis

As with social linguistic analysis, critical linguistic analysis also focuses on individual texts, but with a strong interest in the dynamics of power that surround the text (e.g., Anderson-Gough, Grey, & Robson, 2000; Jackson, 2000). It thus shares the concerns of critical discourse analysis but focuses more closely on the microdynamics of texts. Individual pieces of text are examined to understand how the structures of domination in the local or proximate context are implicated in the text. Witten (1993), for example, examined storytelling from a narrative perspective to understand how stories are used to exert covert control in the workplace. O'Connor (1995) used literary analysis and the study of rhetoric, narrative, and metaphor to explore how organizational change programs are implemented. Kleiner (1998) studied rhetorical strategies to understand how racist ideology is reproduced in conversations.

A good example of this approach is the work of Garnsey and Rees (1996), who used techniques from linguistic studies to examine discourse about women's opportunities in business. They revealed how a variety of linguistic strategies were adopted in four texts that were parts of a discourse that represented inequality as being tied to women's education and training. This discourse diverted attention away from substantial obstacles in the wider context, such as the underuse of women's existing qualifications. Garnsey and Rees's approach can be broadly classified as critical linguistic because they examined different rhetorical strategies adopted by actors to provide accounts, to justify, and to make sense of inequalities in an aspect of social reality—in this case, the distribution of and access to job opportunities. In so doing, these rhetorical strategies contributed to the enactment of inequality and had important political implications.

The authors analyzed four documents pertaining to *Opportunity 2000*, a business-led campaign launched in 1991 in the United Kingdom with government support. The documents included a description of the campaign issued by the promoters and three journal articles referring to the same campaign. These texts were selected because they were considered to represent a "broad spectrum of the ideological positions on the issue of opportunities for women" giving authors "an across and within texts perspective" (Garnsey & Rees, 1996, p. 1046). In focusing intensively on the textual and linguistic dimension of discourse, Garnsey and Rees's study prioritizes text over context in terms of data collection and analysis, although these texts are part of a much broader body of texts related both to equal opportunity and gendered inequality.

The research proceeded in two phases. First, an analysis of the articles revealed discursive themes—such as "goal setting," "training and promotion," and "family-friendly policies"—which served to build a central discourse for women's achievements in companies. This discourse gave "small scope to the acknowledgement of inequalities which stem from common features of social structure" and "little emphasis to proposed remedies" (Garnsey & Rees, 1996, p. 1047). Second, drawing from the work of Barthes and Halliday, Garnsey and Rees explored the linguistic mechanisms and strategies that supported the emerging discourse. The application of the techniques of critical linguistics revealed, for example, a systematic anonymity and an absence of modal verbs. In other words, no subjective viewpoints were present, and the discourse was perceived as objective. The repeated use of passive construction rendered women "passive recipients" of the campaign: Women did not appear or speak anywhere in these texts, and no reference was made to their role or to the initiatives they might take in making known their own needs. The authors concluded that this discourse, as well as the linguistic strategies that supported it, served to reinforce in readers' minds the notion that women were not reaching managerial positions "largely as a result of their own shortcomings" (Garnsey & Rees, p. 1056). In this way, this study provides considerable insight from a detailed microanalysis of texts, using a critical linguistic point of view, into how processes of social construction are bound up with questions of power and domination with regard to women in organizations. Critical linguistics is thus helpful in examining how specific discursive activities and texts help to produce power relations at the local level.

To conclude, the framework shown in Figure 2.1 provides an important tool for understanding the variety of approaches to discourse theory that exist in the literature. Although there are other ways to categorize theoretical approaches, we find this one particularly helpful in understanding the variance in the underlying theoretical perspectives. Even more important, this framework helps researchers to understand their own perspective and design their own studies appropriately, as we discuss further in Chapter 4.

## Empirical Studies in Discourse Analysis

There is more to discourse analysis than just the theoretical perspective adopted by the researcher. There is also the question of the substantive focus of the research. In this section, we provide some tentative answers to the following question: What can be studied from a discourse analysis perspective? We discuss a number of empirical studies that employ discourse analysis, focusing on the phenomena that have been studied, including forms of social control, work and business practices, aspects of identity, as well as issues related to the environment. Our intention is to provide some idea of the range of substantive topics that can be studied, how they can be studied, and what kinds of results can be obtained. Our review is not exhaustive but, rather, indicative of the potential of the method. We feel that such a discussion provides useful insight into what an empirical study actually entails and provides researchers with a useful set of exemplars to think through their own studies.

### Social Control

Modes and techniques of social control are a particularly important focus of study, especially in critical discourse analysis and critical linguistic analysis. In organization and management theory, a critical discourse analytic perspective has been proposed as a way to analyze the practices and techniques that produce and reproduce power relationships within organizations (e.g., Clegg, 1987; Townley, 1993). Critical theorists have argued that the study of the discursive construction of identities and relations can offer a valuable alternative to traditional approaches to the analysis of power and control in organizations. Mumby (1993), for example, argued that stories and other narrative genres contribute to the construction of the social reality that constitutes the lived world of social actors. By portraying and conveying identities, stories help to "linguistically objectify" a social order. Some patterns of interpretation and action are presented as more appropriate, natural, and legitimate than others (Witten, 1993). Empirical examples of this approach include the study of family stories as a discursive practice of social control (Langellier & Peterson, 1993), storytelling as a way to exercise covert control in the workplace (Witten, 1993), and the way in which client service discourse renders managerial controls invisible (Anderson-Gough et al., 2000).

## Studies of Work

The nature of work has also been a focus of several influential studies that fit our definition of discourse analysis. Orr (1996), for example, studied the "practice of experienced technicians maintaining photocopiers for a major US corporation and finds their practice to be a continuous, highly skilled improvisation within a triangular relationship of technician, customer, and machine" (p. 1). Orr focused on the production of narratives by the technicians that made sense of the complex problems encountered as the technicians struggled to keep the machines working and the customers satisfied. Similarly, Jackall (1988) studied the efforts of executives to make sense of the complex and conflictual environment of top management. His study focused particularly on the executives' work to make sense of the ethical dilemmas they faced. Jackall studied their production of narratives to explain and interpret their context and actions. He adopted a critical perspective and focused on the dynamics of power that surround the production of these narratives.

## Business Practice

Organizational researchers have investigated more specific aspects of business practice from a discourse analytic approach. Managerial techniques such as Total Quality Management (De Cock, 1998; Zbaracki, 1998) and accounting conventions (Hoskins & Maeve, 1987), in addition to broader discourses around strategy (Knights & Morgan, 1991) and organizational change (Morgan & Sturdy, 2000; Sillince, 1999), have been studied. Examples include O'Connor's (1995) study of retrospective accounts of a change process in a large corporation, which reveals how narrative choices advanced a concept and practice of change that promoted the interests of particular employees. Researchers have also investigated how business practices become embedded in broader discourses and reflect the distribution of power and interests more broadly across industries and even society (e.g., Knights & Morgan, 1991). Covaleski et al.'s (1998) study discussed above examines business practices such as Management by Objectives (MBO) and mentoring and shows how they exert control over employees. Such studies suggest that the spread of popular management practices, far from being related to their "natural" or "intrinsic" efficiency and rationality, is actually the result of processes of social construction, influenced and shaped by particular actors. Studies adopting a more explicit focus link these activities to attempts by these actors to legitimate their interests and exercise power.

## Discourses of Difference

Many studies have focused on discourses of difference (Wodak, 1996) to explore particular social identities, such as gender, age, and ethnicity. Feminist studies have applied discursive approaches to analyze the construction of occupational gender identity at societal (Garnsey & Rees, 1996; Maile, 1995), organizational (Fletcher, 1998), and individual levels (Gill, 1993a, 1993b; Stokoe, 1998). Another field of application of discourse analysis has been the study of ethnicity and racism. Potter and Wetherell (1987), for example, discussed how "other" ethnicities are constructed to justify racist attitudes. Similarly, van Dijk (1993) showed how narrative analysis—meant as an interpretive deconstruction of stories or retrospective accounts—reveals insight into the construction of ethnicity and race. According to van Dijk, "stories about minorities generally function as complaints by majority group members or as expressions of negative experiences or prejudices about minorities" (p. 125). Although they are essentially expressions of a group's experiences and evaluation, they are presented as "facts" that contribute to the discursive reproduction of racism. Similarly, Kleiner (1998) examined the reproduction of racist discourse through "pseudo-argument" in the talk of undergraduate students. In a related vein, Lutz and Collins (1993) studied the representation of non-Western cultures in National Geographic and the role they play in constructing Americans' understandings of these cultures and their relation to them. Ainsworth (2001) examined how the identity of "mature workers" has been constructed in the public policy forum in Australia, including how gender and age identities interact. This study illustrates how discourse analysis can contribute to an understanding of the fundamentally gendered nature of social constructions of aging as well as its implications for public policy.

## Identity Production

A discourse analytic approach has been the investigation of the production of individual and collective identities within organizational settings. Such research suggests how dominating and emerging discourses in organizations and societies provide a repertoire of concepts, which can be used strategically by members of the community to influence the social construction of identities and to support the institutionalization of practices and patterns of resource distribution (du Gay, 1996). Examples of this field of application range from social identity (e.g., Phillips & Hardy, 1997), occupational identity (e.g., Watson & Bargiela-Chiappina, 1998), corporate identity (e.g., Salzer-Mörling, 1998), and individual identity (e.g., Holmer-Nadeson, 1996). This work investigates the process through which identities are constructed in the interplay of different actors, employing different discursive strategies and resources to establish a definition of identity coherent with particular interests and goals.

## The Environment

Environmental studies—both natural and social—is another field of research where the application of discourse analysis offers a significant contribution. The creation of new concepts, such as toxic waste and endangered species, has led to new understandings of the relationship of business and the environment. Environmental discourse is also an important part of the recent development of an anticapitalism discourse and has led to a strong oppositional discourse to the dominant—and usually positive—globalization discourse. For example, Spicer's (2000) empirical study shows globalization to be a series of contradictory and incomplete economic, cultural geographic, and political "flows." The discourse of globalization fixes the meaning of a loosely related series of shifts in the patterns of social life. Globalization "does not merely describe the world as its advocates seem to pretend, but . . . articulates or reconfigures relations of economic and political power globally" (Dirlik, 1999, p. 39). By exploring historical and organizational texts, Spicer hopes to show how globalization creates particular understandings of the environment in which organizations operate that, in turn, define a series of possibilities and impossibilities with organizational consequences.

Macnaghten (1993) conducted a study on the discursive struggle over the natural environment by examining the construction of the concept of "nature" in a public inquiry. By examining written accounts from a public inquiry concerning a planning application for a landfill site, the author identified a variety of different "discourses of nature" used by the disputants to sustain their arguments and to influence the outcome of the inquiry. In so doing, nature is viewed as socially constructed. Similarly, Welcomer, Gioia, and Kilduff (2000, p. 1175) studied the "clashing discourse between modernity's champions and its skeptics" in the case of a proposal to locate a hazardous waste site in a rural part of Pennsylvania, using participant observation and public documents, such as newspaper articles.

Table 2.1 provides a summary of some of the studies mentioned in this discussion. Our aim is to show some of the phenomena that have been studied using discourse analysis, as well as highlighting diversity in data collection and analysis, and to show where these phenomena are located in terms of the theoretical framework described at the beginning of the chapter.

## A Useful Methodology

In reviewing the literature to prepare to write this chapter, we made three observations. First, we were struck by the variety of theoretical assumptions that empirical studies of discourse analysis can sustain. The idea that collections of texts act to construct the social world provides a surprisingly robust foundation that can support a range of research approaches, as Figure 2.1 demonstrates. Second, this flexibility is even more evident in the discussion of the scope of empirical topics to which discourse analytic methods have been applied. Although there remains scope to develop discourse analysis further, there is already a broad diversity of applications where a discourse perspective has contributed significantly to our understanding of a series of substantive topics such as gender, race, and power. Our review of a selection of these studies highlights this diversity. Finally, we were impressed by the potential of discourse analysis to provide complementary insights to traditional qualitative approaches and to contribute significantly to our understanding to a broad range of organizational, interorganizational, and societal phenomena.

**Table 2.1** Selected Examples of Empirical Discourse Analysis

| Study | Object of analysis | Source of data | Method of analysis | Approach |
|---|---|---|---|---|
| Langellier, K. M., & Peterson, E. E. (1993). Family storytelling as a strategy of social control. In D. Mumby (Ed.), *Narrative and social control: Critical perspectives* (pp. 49–76). Newbury Park, CA: Sage. | Social control | Stories | Narrative analysis | Critical linguistic analysis |
| Ellingson, S. (1995). Understanding the dialectic of discourse and collective action: Public debate and rioting in antebellum Cincinnati. *American Journal of Sociology, 101,* 100–144. | Abolitionism | Archival | Content analysis | Interpretive structuralism |
| Knights, D., & Morgan, G. (1991). "Corporate strategy, organizations, and subjectivity: A critique." *Organization Studies, 12,* 251–273. | Business practice —strategy | Archival (history) | Genealogy | Critical discourse analysis |

| Study | Object of analysis | Source of data | Method of analysis | Approach |
| --- | --- | --- | --- | --- |
| Covaleski et al. (1998). The calculated and the avowed: Techniques of discipline and struggles over identity in the Big Six public accounting firms. *Administrative Science Quarterly, 43,* 293–327. | Business practice —MBO | Ethnography, interviews, direct observation | Ethnography | Critical discourse analysis |
| O'Connor, E. (1995). Paradoxes of participation: Textual analysis and organizational change. *Organization Studies, 16,* 769–803. | Business practice— organizational change | Written accounts of a change process | Literary analysis (rhetoric, narrative, and metaphor) | Social linguistic analysis |
| Watson, T. J., & Bargiela-Chiappina, F. (1998). Managerial sensemaking and occupational identities in Britain and Italy: The role of management magazines in the process of discursive construction. *Journal of Management Studies, 35,* 285–301. | Identity—occupational | Issues of business magazines | Content and linguistic analysis | Social linguistic analysis |

*(Continued)*

**Table 2.1 (Continued)**

| Study | Object of analysis | Source of data | Method of analysis | Approach |
|---|---|---|---|---|
| Wetherell, M., & Potter, J. (1992). *Mapping the language of racism: Discourse and the legitimation of exploitation.* New York: Harvester. | Racism | Interviews | Conversational analysis | Critical linguistic analysis |
| Lutz, C., & Collins, J. (1993). *Reading* National Geographic. Chicago: University of Chicago Press. | Identity—non-Western cultures | Issues of *National Geographic*, archival data, interviews | Photographic analysis | Critical discourse analysis |
| Salzer-Mörling, M. (1998). As God created the earth: A saga that makes sense? In D. Grant, T. Keenoy, & C. Oswick (Eds.), *Discourse and organization* (pp. 104–118). London: Sage. | Identity—corporate | Written and oral accounts of a corporate saga | Narrative analysis | Critical linguistic analysis |

| Study | Object of analysis | Source of data | Method of analysis | Approach |
|---|---|---|---|---|
| Gill, R. (1993a). Justifying injustice: Broadcasters account of inequality in radio. In I. Parker & E. Burman (Eds.), *Discourse analytic research* (pp. 75–93). London: Routledge. | Gender | Interviews | Content and linguistic analysis | Social linguistic analysis |
| Maile, S. (1995). The gendered nature of managerial discourse: The case of a local authority. *Gender, Work, and Organization, 2,* 76–87. | Gender | Archival documentation; interviews | Institutional analysis | Interpretive structuralism |
| Fletcher, J. K. (1998). Relational practice. A feminist reconstruction of work. *Journal of Management Inquiry, 7,* 163–186. | Gender | Ethnographic study; interviews | Ethnography | Critical discourse analysis |

(Continued)

**Table 2.1 (Continued)**

| Study | Object of analysis | Source of data | Method of analysis | Approach |
|---|---|---|---|---|
| van Dijk, T. A. (1993). Stories and racism. In D. Mumby (Ed.), *Narrative and social control* (pp. 121–142). Newbury Park, CA: Sage. | Ethnicity | Stories | Narrative analysis | Critical linguistic analysis |
| Macnaghten, P. (1993). Discourses of nature: Argumentation and power. In I. Parker & E. Burman (Eds.), *Discourse analytic research* (pp. 52–72). London: Routledge. | Environment | Accounts from a public inquiry | Content analysis | Social linguistic analysis |

**Notes**

1. We are indebted to Davide Ravasi for his contribution to this chapter. Much of the material presented here is based on an earlier paper that he coauthored with one of the authors (see Phillips & Ravasi, 1998).

2. For an alternative categorization, see Putnam and Fairhurst (2000).

3. Atlas.ti is one of the many qualitative data-analysis packages currently available.

## 3. OUR RESEARCH PROGRAM

In the last two chapters, we talked generally about discourse analysis and its applications. Our goal was to introduce the general philosophy of discourse analysis and to provide an overview of the range of applications that appear in the current literature. In this chapter, we move closer to home to discuss our own work and to explain why we have adopted a discourse analytic methodology. Focusing on our own work has the advantage of allowing us to go much deeper into the process of conducting discourse analysis and to include many details that show how it was used and what it contributed. In this chapter, we explain why we began using a discourse analytic methodology and show how the methodology contributed to our understanding of various research questions. In the next chapter, we go deeper into the practicalities of discourse analysis when we use our work to discuss the steps to be taken in designing and conducting a discourse analytic research project.

We have been engaged in a series of discourse studies in a variety of settings, including (a) refugee systems in Canada, Denmark, and the United Kingdom; (b) the whale-watching industry in British Columbia; (c) the Canadian HIV/AIDS treatment domain; (d) an aid organization operating in the West Bank and Gaza; and (e) employment service organizations in western Canada (see Table 3.1 for details of individual studies). This program of research is an offshoot of an earlier research project involving a critical study of interorganizational collaboration. In the earlier research, we were interested in the role that power played in creating and shaping collaborations and in how the effects of collaboration, often presented in the organizational and management literature as a "good" thing, were often intensely political and highly disadvantageous for some participants. Furthermore, as we explored the political aspects of collaboration, it became clear that it was not only the relationships between collaborating organizations that were important, but also the impact of the collaboration on other relationships in the larger system.[1] We subsequently explored how relationships between organizations—conflict as well as cooperation—influenced the distribution of power among organizations and other actors in various systems (e.g., Hardy, 1994; Hardy et al., 1998b; Hardy & Phillips, 1998; Lawrence & Hardy, 1999). These studies are not all located in a single quadrant of Figure 2.1, or even only on the critical side of the continuum. Although many of our studies are critical, and all are discursive, different studies are located in different quadrants (we return to this point later). This leads to an important observation about discourse analysis. Although Figure 2.1 is useful in categorizing individual research studies, it should not be seen as categorizing *researchers*. In fact, moving from one quadrant to another is often required to deal with different kinds of research questions. Changing the focus of the research often leads to a subsequent study, which may be located in a different quadrant from previous work: As researchers try to understand different aspects of the phenomenon in question, they can expect to adopt different frames. We find this to be an exciting aspect of discourse analysis because it allows us the freedom to examine very different aspects of social reality from a consistent social constructivist framework.

So why did we adopt a discursive perspective to begin with? The answer is simple: We needed a methodology that would allow us to investigate the role of social construction in collaboration. When we began investigating collaboration, our approach was critical, not discursive. Before long, however, we became aware that although a critical perspective helped to explain the social and political nature of the relationships between and within organizations (i.e., how they worked), it did not help us to understand how they came into being or to identify the processes of social construction that held them in place. As we started to consider these more fundamental questions, a number of specific issues began to emerge that led us to adopt a more explicitly discursive approach. They relate to the reasons for doing discourse analysis that we identified in Chapter 1. In a general sense, we had become increasingly interested in how the linguistic turn might be incorporated into the study of organizations. In addition, we were interested in what was for us a new topic of study—identity—that warranted a discursive approach. We also wanted to develop our existing critical perspective and explore the political effects of discourse. Finally, we saw the potential of a discursive perspective in building on and complementing other bodies of theoretical work. We present these reasons in more detail below.

## Studying Identity

One reason for using discourse analysis was the emergence of concepts that we had not previously considered but that, it became clear, were crucial to our understanding of the complex interorganizational relationships in our studies. Identity, in particular, was central—not a traditional view of identity as a stable, essential characteristic but, rather, a fragmented, fluid and ambiguous identity that changed over time with interesting implications.

The issue of identity first became evident in our work on refugees (Box 3.1). Refugee determination is often presented as a quasi-legal process during which the available evidence is examined to "reveal" whether an individual is a refugee. From a discourse analytic perspective, however, things looked very different. Rather than a highly rational process that separated "real" and "fraudulent" refugees, the identity of a refugee was contested, unstable, and discursively constructed. Furthermore, we found that actors in the refugee system had a stake in these different identities and acted discursively to support them. For example, the government juxtaposed "political refugees" against the "economic migrants" that had to be unmasked by their determination procedures. The white-led nongovernmental organizations (NGOs) that spoke on behalf of refugees defined refugees as needy "clients" to whom they, as professionals, could dispense services. The refugee-based organizations constructed refugees as fully functioning and equal "members" of society who were willing and able to organize themselves.

By using discourse analysis to "unpack" these competing refugee identities, we were able to provide insight into a number of aspects of the refugee determination system. First, in discursively evoking and drawing on particular refugee identities, *organizational* identities were also constructed. The government's role was to protect the public and stop the arrival of illegal refugees. One NGO viewed its mission as dispensing services to needy clients, whereas another saw itself as providing services but also representing a refugee constituency. The refugee organization saw itself as fighting against these other organizations to empower its members. These identities shaped organizational practice. So, for example, the service provider found it difficult to engage in meaningful consultation with its "clients" because

(Text continues on page 46)

**Table 3.1** Summary of the Authors' Empirical Discourse Publications

| Publication | Research site | Research object | Data | Findings |
|---|---|---|---|---|
| Phillips, N., & Hardy, C. (1997). Managing multiple identities: Discourse, legitimacy and resources in the UK refugee system. *Organization, 4,* 159–186. | Refugee system in the United Kingdom | Refugee identities | Interviews, organizational and government texts | Organizations engage in discursive strategies to produce particular refugee identities and, in so doing, construct refugee and other identities |
| Hardy, C., & Phillips, N. (1999). No joking matter: Discursive struggle in the Canadian refugee system. *Organization Studies, 20,* 1–24. | Refugee system in Canada | Refugee (and other) identities | Cartoons | Societal level discourses provide resources that actors may use in strategies to construct identities |
| Hardy, C., Phillips, N., & Clegg, S. R. (2001). Reflexivity in organization and management studies: A study of the production of the research "subject." *Human Relations, 54,* 3–32. | Refugee system in Canada | Our own research on refugees | Published articles, journal texts | The researcher and the research community discursively produce the research subject |

| Publication | Research site | Research object | Data | Findings |
|---|---|---|---|---|
| Lawrence, T., & Phillips, N. (1997). *From Moby Dick to Free Willy: The discursive construction of a cultural industry*. Paper presented at the conference on Research Perspectives on the Management of Cultural Industries, Stern School of Management, New York University, New York. | Whale watching in Canada | Institutional field | Interviews, organizational and cultural texts | Change in macrolevel discourses make possible the development of institutional fields that are shaped by institutional entrepreneurs |
| Lawrence, T., Phillips, N., & Hardy, C. (1999a). Watching whale-watching: A relational theory of organizational collaboration. *Journal of Applied Behavioral Science, 35*, 479–502. | Whale watching in Canada | Collaboration | Interviews, organizational and cultural texts | Collaboration depends on an ongoing process of discursive negotiation about the meaning of issues, interests, and representation |
| Hardy, C., Lawrence, T., & Phillips, N. (1998b). Talking action: Conversations, narrative and action in interorganizational collaboration. In D. Grant, T. Keenoy, & C. Oswick (Eds.), *Discourse and organization* (pp. 65–83). London: Sage. | Employment services in Canada | Collaboration | Interviews, participant observation | Collaboration is constructed discursively through the construction of emotion, identity, and cultural skills |

(*Continued*)

**Table 3.1 (Continued)**

| Publication | Research site | Research object | Data | Findings |
|---|---|---|---|---|
| Hardy, C., Palmer, I., & Phillips, N. (2000). Discourse as a strategic resource. *Human Relations*, 53(9), 7–28. | NGO in the West Bank and Gaza | Discursive strategies | Interviews, organizational texts | Discourse becomes a strategic resource when discursive activity is grounded in the particular context in which it is enacted |
| Maguire, S., Phillips, N., & Hardy, C. (2001a). When "Silence = Death" keep talking: Trust, control, and the discursive construction of identity in the Canadian HIV/AIDS treatment domain. *Organization Studies*, 22, 287–312. | Canadian HIV/AIDS treatment domain | Trust and identity | Interviews, observation, archival texts | Trust is achieved through the discursive construction of identities that confer predictability and goodwill within the context of a shared myth |
| Maguire, S., Hardy, C., & Lawrence, T. (2001b). *Peripheral actors as institutional entrepreneurs in the elaboration of institutional fields: HIV/AIDS treatment advocacy in Canada.* Paper presented at the conference of the European Group on Organization Studies, Lyons, France. | Canadian HIV/AIDS treatment domain | Institutional entrepreneurship | Interviews, observation, archival texts | Institutional entrepreneurship is achieved through discursive moves to construct identity |

**Box 3.1**
**Example: Study of Refugee Systems**

Refugee systems determine the status of refugee claimants and carry out the settlement of those granted asylum. They encompass the formation and implementation of policies and practices that relate to the rights of individuals to claim asylum, the procedures whereby claimants are awarded asylum, and the support provided once asylum is awarded. Three broad groupings of stakeholders are involved: government, NGOs, and refugees. Our study compared the refugee systems in three countries—Canada, the United Kingdom, and Denmark. It explored how different constructions of refugee identities influenced the determination decisions whereby individual asylum seekers are found to be (or not to be) refugees and are granted (or denied) asylum in another country.

We conducted qualitative case studies of the refugee systems in these three countries with open-ended interviews with 81 civil servants, politicians, NGO officials, refugees in government, the refugee councils, other NGOs, and refugee organizations. We examined a series of texts from different organizations, newspapers, and government to explore refugee discourses. They included government statistics, annual reports and minutes from annual meetings, published documentation, Hansard reports of parliamentary speeches in the United Kingdom and Canada, and newspaper articles. In addition, we analyzed a series of editorial cartoons on refugees and immigrants in Canadian newspapers as indicators of the broader societal-level discourse around immigration. Data collection was carried out between 1990 and 1995.

We found a high degree of discursive struggle around central concepts pertaining to the refugee system, particularly between human rights and sovereignty and between paternalism and empowerment, which produced contradictory views concerning refugee identities, including "political refugee," "economic migrant," as well as refugees as "clients" or as a "constituency." Although the official story suggested that individuals were determined to be refugees as a result of examining the "facts" that determined their "true" status, it was clear that the process was rather more ambiguous and tenuous. In particular,

---

**Box 3.1** *(continued)*

different refugee identities, constituted through the specific discursive activities of different organizations as well as through broader societal-level discourses, shaped the way in which the system operated. In addition, actors engaged in discursive activities to influence the identities of refugees and other actors. In this way, the research setting offered considerable insight into how discursive power operated through the construction of identity, the way in which individual and organizational identities informed each other, and the link between organizational identities and organizational practice. We were also able to show how broader discourses provide resources on which actors can draw in their attempts to act strategically. Finally, we used the study to examine our role—as researchers—in the social construction processes, in particular, how the way in which we write and publish our research produces the research subject. In other words, rather than reveal a "true" subject through our research endeavors, we produce subjects that conform to institutionalized practices in our respective disciplines, which may then be "fed back" to the world in which they were observed.

*Note:* This research was carried out with Tom Lawrence, School of Business, University of Victoria, Canada.

---

its procedures were predicated on refugees being passive recipients, not equal partners. The second NGO, on the other hand, introduced a series of mechanisms to give voice to its constituency, which were then used by refugees to influence and shape the organization and its policies. The refugee organization refused to cooperate with the NGOs, much to their frustration and amazement—as a small, impoverished organization, they could not understand why it would not want to cooperate with them. An organizational identity that sees refugees not as silent clients but as a vocal and capable constituency that is being marginalized, however, leads to an organization that is not going to collaborate with established agencies, regardless of how their interests might appear to overlap.

Second, in highlighting the discursive struggle around identities, we were also able to provide a better understanding of power. Traditional views of power—as derived from resource dependencies or formal authority—would suggest that the government was the dominant stakeholder and the refugee organization was virtually powerless. A discursive view, however, reveals that power can be exercised by creating meaning for social objects and that certain identities are able to have an influence—even organizations that lack traditional power. So the refugee-based organization, through its construction of an identity as the only legitimate voice for refugees as well as its confrontational relations with NGOs that tried to usurp its role, was able to secure voice. It had a profound influence in pushing more established NGOs to change their practices and increase refugee participation. Accordingly, an organization almost devoid of traditional power resources had a significant impact on other organizations through its use of discursive power (Phillips & Hardy, 1997).

In our work on the development of commercial whale watching (Box 3.2), we found that the way in which the identity of a whale was constructed was an important precursor of the industry's development. Society's conceptualization of whales has changed profoundly over the last 150 years. Animals that were once considered horrifying beasts—consider Melville's *Moby Dick*—have been reconstructed into almost mythical creatures deserving of our respect and admiration—the *Free Willy* of the three recent Hollywood films. To understand the development of commercial whale watching as a tourist activity, it is critical to understand the radical changes that have occurred in macrodiscourses, particularly representations of the whale, which emerged at the intersection of regulatory, scientific, ecological, and popular culture discourses about whales. A whale-watching industry depends on a "Free Willy" identity of the whale; Moby Dick poses significant problems for this particular niche of ecotourism because spectators are unlikely to be willing to board small boats to get close to a human-eating monster. By exploring the effects of changing identities in the case of whales, we were able to show how institutional fields depend on macro-cultural discourses. In other words, to understand the construction of an institutional field, we must pay some attention to the broader context in which it exists and the fact that individuals seeking to influence the development of an institutional field—institutional entrepreneurs—are constrained and enabled by discourses that exist outside the specific field (Lawrence & Phillips, 1997).

**Box 3.2**

**Example: Study of British Columbia Whale-Watching Industry**

Whale watching in British Columbia cuts across a range of traditional industries and activities. It consists of professional and amateur whale watchers who watch whales for fun, research, or commercial purposes. The industry has been growing rapidly since its birth in the 1970s and is made up of operators of small boats in the lower Vancouver Island area and of larger boats in northern parts of Vancouver Island. In addition, a number of marine research organizations study the behavior, habitat, and movements of the whales. The commercial whale watchers and the researchers exchange information on the whereabouts of the whales, on their behavior, and on the well-being of particular members of the whale population. There are also a range of other, less central actors, including amateur whale watchers; related industries such as sea plane companies (who often spot whales and pass on the information), ferry companies, and fishing boat companies; and various regulators such as the government of British Columbia, the Canadian and U.S. Coast Guards, and various travel and tourism boards and associations.

Data collection included a series of 17 tape-recorded, semistructured interviews with key actors in the field carried out in 1995–1996 and a wide range of textual materials such as company brochures, meeting agendas, books, and articles of various kinds on the industry. Data also came from a range of scholarly texts, the Internet Movie Database, and Microsoft's Cinemania CD-ROM, with more detailed data then being collected through a variety of sources, including film-oriented Internet newsgroups, personal communications, and watching the movies ourselves.

We found that the emergence of a commercial whale-watching industry in North America was only possible because of broad changes in the conceptualization of whales—from whales as "dangerous monsters" to whales as "intelligent individuals"—that occurred through complex processes involving multiple discourses and which then provided a space within which the institutional entrepreneurs worked to influence the field. We also found that interorganizational collaboration is not a narrowly circumscribed activity but is, in fact, a means of influencing the larger field of which it is a part. In this way, our work was able to provide a broader and more contextualized understanding of collaboration and to show how it affects and is affected by the broader organizational field in which it occurs, as well as showing the links between discursive activity and institutional entrepreneurship. We also developed a framework based on a discursive approach that helped to explain the dynamics of collaboration, particularly between researchers and tour operators, in the whale-watching industry. Understanding collaboration discursively reveals the nature of the collaborative process, particularly how participants negotiate the issues that are to be addressed by the collaboration, the interests that are relevant to the collaboration and legitimacy of potential stakeholders, and the actors who should represent these legitimate interests. In this way, we are able to understand how collaboration can be managed in terms of identifying the antecedents that make it possible, the dynamics by which it occurs, and the outcomes that it produces.

*Note:* This research was carried out with Tom Lawrence, School of Business, University of Victoria, Canada.

Our study of the Canadian HIV/AIDS treatment domain (Box 3.3) also hinged on an understanding of identity. We were particularly interested in how an ongoing collaboration between community members and pharmaceutical companies had been created and sustained, given that these two groups—activists and employees—had previously spent most of their time in direct conflict with each other and that both parties still held very different goals and values. To understand how the collaboration came about, we explored the way in which the advent of AIDS in the 1980s had undermined established identities in the medical treatment domain. It had caused a knowledge and treatment vacuum with a public display of scientific uncertainty and institutional impotence in the face of this new crisis and, as a result, traditional assumptions about who was knowledgeable and who could be trusted started to erode. For example, not only did physicians *not* have the expertise to deal with this new challenge, some were even unwilling to try to treat AIDS patients. Another change concerned the identity of individuals with the disease, who began to reject the identity of "patient" and instead defined themselves as PWAs—people living with AIDS. In addition, PWAs began to demand and exercise more control over their treatment, and a new identity of "AIDS activist" emerged, individuals who

**Box 3.3**

**Example: Study of the Canadian HIV/AIDS Treatment Domain**

This study focused on the relation between pharmaceutical companies and the HIV/AIDS community in Canada. The treatment of people living with AIDS (PWAs) generates huge profits for a variety of pharmaceutical companies, which are primarily concerned with commercial and profit-making considerations. At the same time, the aim of PWAs is to secure quick access to safe and effective treatments. In the past, this has led to open conflict between community members and pharmaceutical companies. More recently, however, these two groups have been working together—initially through companies' informal consultation of knowledgeable community members and, subsequently, in more formalized venues as companies established their own community advisory boards to exchange information about treatment efficacy and safety, review research protocols, and negotiate compassionate access programs. The most recent phase of consultation in Canada has been the creation of a new national organization— the Canadian Treatment Advocates Council (CTAC), which was officially launched in January 1997, bringing together more than 15 regional and national HIV/AIDS community organizations and eight major pharmaceutical companies.

We studied the creation of CTAC by interviewing key individuals involved in its creation, as well as other actors in the field, between 1995 and 2000. We also collected documents from community organizations, companies, and CTAC itself, as well as more general information on HIV/AIDS. We participated in some of the meetings that led to CTAC, as well as the 1996 International Conference on AIDS in Vancouver.

This study shows the deconstruction and reconstruction of identities as the discourse of the HIV/AIDS treatment domain in Canada evolved. Expert and trustworthy doctors lost both expertise and trust as they struggled to deal with the new disease. Passive patients became people living with HIV/AIDS and activists. Activists became treatment advocates, and pill-pushing, profiteering companies became compassionate and consultative partners. This, in turn, helped us to show how a collaboration between former adversaries was created and sustained, as well as to explain the form that the collaboration took and the way in which it developed. The study allowed us to explore the way in which peripheral actors can play an important role in fostering institutional change, especially through discursive activities that include managing identities in ways that secure these actors a voice, translating diverse interests through discursive framing that appeals to conflicting stakeholders, and entrenching new practices in organizational forms. The study also provides insight into the discursive foundations of identification-based trust, providing more information on the dynamics of trust and suggesting how trusting relationships can be created. It also shows how discussions of control should be extended to include the concept of discursively constructed identities. Power is embedded in identity and, by engaging in discursive action, actors can create identities through which they are able to exercise control over others' behavior.

*Note:* This research was carried out with Tom Lawrence, School of Business, University of Business, University of Victoria, Canada, and Steve Maguire, Faculty of Management, McGill University, Montreal, Canada.

directly and openly confronted medical, pharmaceutical, and regulatory organizations. At this stage, it was clear that identities were changing, but it was not clear how "activists" would come to collaboration with the "profiteering" pharmaceutical companies they generally despised. We then investigated further and found evidence of another new identity—"treatment advocate"—expert, professional PWAs who were willing to work with pharmaceutical companies to improve treatment. We also found that the pharmaceutical companies started to redefine themselves as "partners"— able and willing to work with the community. Only with these changes in the construction of identities was collaboration in the HIV/AIDS treatment domain possible. We also saw how actors engaged, individually and collectively, in identity work to position themselves as participants in the collaboration and how individuals who could not construct themselves appropriately—such as HIV-positive drug users, the HIV-negative community, and employees from a particular pharmaceutical company that had a bad reputation in the community—were excluded from the collaboration. This, in turn, had important implications for the activities and goals of the collaboration. (Maguire, Phillips, & Hardy, 2001).

In summary, as identity emerged as an important topic in our research, we began to adopt a more explicitly discursive approach, both epistemologically and methodologically. Focusing our attention on the discursive processes that constitute identities made the value of this perspective clear. Identity in this reconceptualized, nonessential form is currently in vogue in a number of different disciplines. Our own work, as well as the work of others, shows how particular constructions of identity shape collaborations, organizations, industries, and fields. We cannot understand processes of organizing unless we understand identity—and understand it from a discursive perspective because reified views of identity do not help researchers capture the fluidity of social life.

## Revitalizing Our Critical Approach

A second reason why our work became more explicitly discursive stemmed from our ongoing concern with power. Originally, we had focused on the politics of collaboration using a traditionally critical orientation. Aware of the dangers of reifying phenomena such as "organizations," we started to examine more explicitly how organizations, collaborations, domains, and fields could be conceptualized as fluid, unfinished, fragile relationships that were made meaningful and "real" through discourse. In this way, we started to explore the strategies whereby actors used discursive resources to produce certain outcomes, as well as the way in which other actors attempted to resist these activities. In this way, discourse analysis helped to develop our critical perspective in new directions.

For example, in our study of Mère et Enfant (Box 3.4), when we learned of the threats by the security forces to interrogate and imprison employees and the subsequent actions taken by the manager, it was clear that we were encountering a major disturbance in the "production" of a local NGO, as well as a subsequent reversal back to an international NGO, all within a relatively limited time frame. This allowed us to examine discursive activity from a strategic perspective. In so doing, we were able to track how the organization had "become" a local NGO as a result of discursive changes such as setting up a steering committee, introducing an Arabic version of the organization's name, and through a series of written documents. We were also able to observe how the manager deliberately invoked a counterstrategy of discursive moves—disbanding the steering committee and sending out a series of memos and letters invoking symbols and narratives associated with

**Box 3.4**
**Example: Study of Mère et Enfant (Palestine)**

Mère et Enfant[a] is a European-based international NGO that works on behalf of needy children worldwide. We studied one particular "branch," Mère et Enfant (Palestine), which operates in the West Bank and Gaza, employing about 60 Palestinians, and is managed by an expatriate. This region comprises densely populated areas that are mainly rural and poor. Half the population is under 14 years old, and infant mortality rates are high. Mère et Enfant's main emphasis is on child nutrition. It provides clinical services, education, and outreach services; it also provides policy advice and conducts research on nutritional status and other matters related to the health of Palestinian children.

We carried out 14 semistructured interviews in 1997 with employees of the organization, local members of the steering committee, members of the Palestinian Ministry of Health, and representatives of other organizations with whom Mère et Enfant worked. We also collected and analyzed a range of texts including all organizational newsletters and brochures, as well as letters, faxes, memos, organizational charts, year-end reports, minutes of meetings, funding proposals, and other documents.

Mère et Enfant was in the process of "localizing" its activities, a process by which operations previously administered and funded by the international NGO are transformed into a local NGO. The local NGO is typically managed by a steering committee comprised of representatives from the local community. The manager had been implementing a series of preparatory changes that included restructuring and some redundancies. He had also arranged a meeting of individuals whom he thought might become members of the prospective steering committee, although decision making remained under his control and Mère et Enfant (Palestine) was still part of the larger organization. Although lacking any formal authority, these individuals met in his absence to discuss some recently announced redundancies and issued a statement that the employees should be reinstated. By this time, in the eyes of many Palestinians, including the security forces, the organization was now a local NGO as a result of discursive

---

**Box 3.4** *(continued)*

moves such as the creation of a steering committee. As a local NGO, its employees were left without the political protection afforded by the status of an international agency and were immediately subjected to harassment by the local security forces. To protect his employees, the manager engaged in a number of discursive activities designed to reestablish the status of the organization as an international agency with political connections and financial clout. He sent out a series of memos and letters and disbanded the steering committee, and as a result, he eventually received reassurances from members of the Palestinian National Authority that employees were safe from further intervention by the security forces. The organization had once again "become" an international NGO. In this way, the events that occurred in this study have allowed us to explore the use of discourse as a strategic resource and to identify the ways in which organizations can be created and changed by invoking different discourses and changing meaning.

*Note:* a. The name of the organization has been changed.
This research was carried out with Ian Palmer, School of Management, University of Technology, Sydney, Australia

---

an international NGO—to curtail that localization process and avoid further intervention by the security forces (Hardy, Palmer, & Phillips, 2000). In this way, we were able to identify some of the discursive foundations on which seemingly "solid" entities such as organizations are built; to show how, by changing this symbolic and linguistic infrastructure, organizational change is achieved as new meanings are created; and to cast light on how an organization's environment changes as new subject positions are established—sometimes unexpectedly—as the result of new meanings.

In summary, we found that an explicitly discursive approach proved useful in exploring the political and strategic effects of discursive moves. This was reinforced by findings of our other studies, such as the strategies of actors in refugee systems to discursively produce refugee identities that would reinforce and consolidate their power in the domain (Phillips & Hardy, 1997) and the ability of peripheral actors in the Canadian HIV/AIDS treatment domain to use discourse to leverage identities in ways that enabled them to change the domain (Maguire, Hardy, & Lawrence, 2001).

In this way, we have been able to complement our view of power based on traditional critical assumptions (e.g., Hardy, 1985) with a perspective that emphasizes the role of discourse, identity, power, and knowledge (see Alvesson & Deetz, 2000). Accordingly, we concur with other researchers who have argued that the future of organization and management theory lies in work at the interface of these two meta-theories (e.g., Clegg & Hardy, 1996a). "Without considering postmodern themes, critical theory easily becomes unreflective . . . without incorporating some measure of critical theory . . . postmodernism simply becomes esoteric" (Alvesson & Deetz, 2000, p. 107).

## A New Perspective on Existing Theoretical Debates

A third motivation behind our use of discourse theory and analysis stemmed from our wish to build on and complement other theoretical bodies of work. It became clear that a discursive perspective offered considerable potential to contribute to theoretical debates in other streams of literature. For example, we realized that the structuration of institutional fields (DiMaggio & Powell, 1983) and the organization of interorganizational domains (McCann, 1983) depend partly on discursive activities. In this way, we have been able to build on both institutional theory and domain theory by understanding how discursive activities constitute the common understandings, rules, and practices that form the institutions that define a particular field, or the issues that define a domain (Lawrence, Phillips, & Hardy, 1999a, 1999b; Phillips, Lawrence, & Hardy, 2000). Using a discursive approach in our studies of whale watching (Lawrence & Phillips, 1997) and the Canadian HIV/AIDS domain (Maguire, Hardy, & Lawrence, 2001) to explore institutional entrepreneurship further extends insights into institutional theory. Institutional entrepreneurship is a concept that has been introduced into institutional theory as researchers have sought to address issues of agency. So far, however, the activities of institutional entrepreneurship have not been well defined. By focusing on the specific discursive activities of individuals, we have been able to identify specific processes that have led to institutional change. They include drawing on different identities that locate actors—even relatively powerless ones—in positions from which they can influence the field, the ability to frame diverse arguments in ways that cut across sectional interests, and the entrenchment of new practices by discursively embedding them in organizational texts. By combining discourse analysis with institutional theory, we have been able to develop a model of institutional change.

Another study in which we have tried to build on existing theory is in our research on employment service organizations in Western Canada (Box 3.5). We used the work of microsociologist Randall Collins (1981) on conversational activity, supplementing it with narrative analysis (e.g., Cobb & Rifkin, 1991) to show how, through the production of meaning, collective action is generated. Microsociologists such as Collins contend that the social world exists neither as an objective entity nor as a set of meanings that people carry in their heads, but in repeated actions of communicating. Collins conceived of these communicating actions as conversations that generate collective action through the *activity* of talking. Narrative theory tells us that action is also generated through the content of talk by "defining characters, sequencing plots, and scripting actions" (Boje, 1995, p. 1000). Thus, we derived a discursive approach to generating collective action by combining and building on these two bodies of theory in a way that has practical implications for collaborative activity through the management of emotion, skills, and identity (Hardy, Lawrence, & Phillips, 1998).

A third theoretical area to which we have applied discourse analysis has been trust. The literature on trust has identified a variety of different forms (e.g., Lewicki & Bunker, 1995). One form of trust that has not received a lot of attention is identification-based trust (compared with calculus-based and knowledge-based trust). It involves goodwill as well as predictability in behavior and hence is considered a "strong" form of trust (Hardy, Phillips, & Lawrence, 1998; Shapiro, Sheppard, & Cheraskin, 1992). We explored how this form of trust might be discursively generated. Prescriptions for generating identification-based trust have, in the past, stressed the importance of a common shared collective identity (Lewicki & Bunker, 1995; Shapiro et al., 1992). Yet our analysis of the HIV/AIDS treatment domain suggested that trust can also be generated between actors who do not share an identity if actors can credibly construct themselves and others as possessing particular identities that lead actors to exhibit goodwill and to tolerate situations of exposure to opportunism. The generation and maintenance of this form of trust is therefore intimately tied to the construction of identities (Maguire, Phillips, & Hardy, 2001).

In summary, we have found the application of discourse analysis particularly helpful in contributing to other theoretical literatures. First, it provides the theoretical and methodological tools to add an interesting perspective to

**Box 3.5**
**Example: Study of Employment Service Organizations in**
**Western Canada**

The Community Partners[a] are a group of 13 organizations that provide employment services to the unemployed, including counseling, training, and support, in a midsized Canadian city. The group includes publicly funded postsecondary educational institutions, private-sector organizations and not-for-profit organizations that range in size from fewer than 20 employees to more than 3,000. The Community Partners was formed when the manager of one of the primary funding agencies called together all of the organizations with which it had contracts to provide employment services. He wanted these agencies to work together to serve his agency's clients—individuals collecting employment insurance living in a particular geographic area—more effectively. He also hoped that the group would serve as an information conduit between the Employment Office and the wider employment services community. The Community Partners met monthly for 2-hour meetings during a period of approximately 18 months, but with little result. Finally, a collaboration workshop was instigated at the initiative of the employment manager and one of the partners, partly due to the lack of progress. It involved the Community Partners meeting for 3.5 days spread over a 6-week period.

Data collection for this case study included preworkshop interviews with each of the 13 participants, extensive note taking by a research assistant during the 3.5-day workshop and an open-ended survey at the workshop's close. One of the researchers facilitated the collaboration workshop itself. The initial interviews with the representatives of the participating organizations identified the critical issues facing each of them. A diversity of opinions surfaced regarding the importance and potential benefits of the partnership: Some participants viewed the collaboration and the workshop with skepticism, wondering what benefits could possibly justify more than 3 days away from their regular organizational duties; others saw tremendous potential for the group as a social and political force; still others looked forward to forging closer personal and professional

---

**Box 3.5** *(continued)*

links with the other participants. The follow-up interviews found that as a result of the workshop, members moved much further toward generating collaborative action than had previously been achieved. They founded a new organization; developed its mission and vision; articulated, prioritized, and set dates for major goals; and assigned teams to each goal.

The study highlights the role of conversations in generating collaborative action. Drawing on both microsociological approaches and narrative theory, we examined in detail how conversations in the workshop discursively produced an identity, skills, and emotions that facilitated the collaboration, thus building a model of how collaboration can be achieved through discursive means.

*Note:* a. The name of the group has been changed.
This research was carried out with Tom Lawrence, School of Business, University of Victoria, Canada.

---

several ongoing debates. In this way, some of the gaps in these theories can be addressed, such as the difficulty that institutional theory has in dealing with agency (Tolbert & Zucker, 1996) or the problem in understanding how trust can be created between actors who do not share common values or who are not familiar with each other (Hardy, Phillips, & Lawrence, 1998). Second, although discourse analysis is sometimes criticized for being abstract and theoretical, it shows potential for more practical applications because it allows researchers to tease out specific discursive activities. In this way, we can start, for example, to see how discourse theory might translate into practice. Finally, in a field where pluralism is increasingly called for (Clegg & Hardy, 1996b; Kaghan & Phillips, 1998), a new perspective can be a more significant contribution than work focusing on the incremental development of existing perspectives. A fresh eye often leads to more innovative thinking.

## Why We Use Discourse Analysis

Three particular reasons have motivated our adoption of a discourse analytic methodology. First, our interest in identity led us to focus increasingly on the role of language and social construction and, in turn, to discourse analysis.

Second, our interest in power and in moving beyond more established critical views of power prompted an interest in processes of social construction and in a critical version of discourse analysis. Finally, once we began to use discourse analysis, we began to see other opportunities to contribute to ongoing discussions in the literature by adding a different view to more traditional theoretical approaches. These three specific reasons overlay a general interest in the linguistic turn that permeates our recent work. In this way, four of the five reasons for adopting discourse analysis that we discussed in Chapter 1 have played an important role in our initial adoption and continued use of the methodology.

Although not everyone will necessarily share our particular reasons for adopting a discourse analytic methodology, they nonetheless provide an excellent example of the contributions that discourse analysis can make if adopted by other researchers in their own work. An interest in a particular theoretical or substantive topic, a desire to look at a familiar topic in a new way, or an interest in social construction are among the important reasons that warrant the adoption of discourse analysis. Researchers considering adopting a discourse analytic approach should carefully consider why they are adopting the methodology and what benefits that it will provide. This is an important part of designing a study because it provides an initial set of concerns to guide the design process and will be critical to the process of writing up the study when the researcher must defend the choice of methodology to reviewers.

**Note**

1. By system, we refer to the larger arena in which collaboration takes place, which may include an industry or sector or, more specifically, a domain (Gray, 1989; Laumann & Knoke, 1987) or field (Bourdieu, 1993; DiMaggio & Powell, 1983; Warren, Rose, & Bergunder, 1974).

# 4. THE CHALLENGES OF DISCOURSE ANALYSIS

In the preface to this book, we argued that discourse analysis is both a perspective and a method. It is a perspective in that it brings with it a particular view of social phenomena as constituted through structured sets of texts of various kinds. It is a method in that it is a way of approaching data collection and analysis. In the two previous chapters, we focused on the former aspect—discourse analysis as a perspective. We defined discourse analysis, provided a rationale for its use, and discussed our motivations for using it in our own research. In this sense, we have focused on the philosophy of discourse analysis.

In this chapter, we change direction and explore some of the more practical issues that face researchers who want to use discourse analysis in their work. We identify some of the major challenges that arise at each stage of a study and discuss some solutions. Some of the challenges remain relatively intractable, and each new study requires the development of new, individual ways of tackling the issue; others are less troublesome because solutions that have been developed in other studies can be readily applied. Our goal in this chapter is to highlight the challenges that arise in doing discourse analysis, including the development of research questions, selecting a site, collecting data, analyzing data, and writing up the study. To help researchers design a study, we have included a set of questions that they should ask themselves as they plan their research. Although it may not always be possible to come up with a complete answer before beginning a study, simply asking oneself the questions goes a long way toward helping researchers tackle the challenges of discourse analysis.

## Developing a Research Question

Designing a research study is as much an art as it is a science. A good research study combines scientific methods and theoretical savvy with a creative turn that surprises and interests a community of scholars. As with any creative process, there is no single best way to approach this process. We have found that beginning with an explicit research question is often an effective first step, however. A good research question provides a frame for making decisions about data collection and analysis, explains the motivation behind the study, and provides guidance for writing it up. This is not to say that an explicit research question is always required before beginning a study. In fact, some authors even argue against beginning with a theoretical frame at all. We have found a clear research question to be very helpful in designing and carrying out a study, however, and particularly useful for less experienced researchers.

The nature of the research question will obviously vary from study to study because it depends on a range of factors that vary from researcher to researcher and topic to topic. In our experience, there are four factors that are important in shaping the research question: the research philosophy of the researcher, the nature of the object of study, the particular body of theory on which the researcher is drawing, and the particular contribution that the researcher hopes to make. We consider each of these factors in turn.

## The Researcher's Philosophy

Research questions begin with research philosophies. Or, to say it another way, research questions grow out of the set of basic assumptions about the topic of study held by the researcher. At its most fundamental, the choice of discourse analysis itself reflects a particular philosophy, in this case, a strong social constructivist epistemology. Within this broad frame, however, researchers' philosophies will obviously vary. One way to conceptualize this diversity, and to think through how philosophy might influence the research question, is to locate the research project according to the matrix in Figure 2.1. This figure reflects the basic interests and assumptions of the researcher within a broader discourse analytic framework. To illustrate this, in Figure 4.1 we locate some of our own studies according to this framework and, in the remainder of this section, we show how our research questions differed accordingly.

First, consider our study of the British refugee system (Phillips & Hardy, 1997; Box 3.1 in Chapter 3). In this study, we examined the way in which organizations used power to discursively shape the conceptualization of a refugee in ways that protected their interests. Our focus was on the broad context of the refugee determination system in the United Kingdom, the conflicting organizational interests that existed, and the unequal way that power was distributed among organizations in the system. Our emphasis was, as a result, on using an explicitly critical approach to discourse analysis to understand the context of refugee determination (see Figure 4.1). Consequently, our research question made explicit reference to both power and context: *How do interested organizations work to change the concept of a refugee and influence the production of refugees as objects, thereby influencing the determination system?*

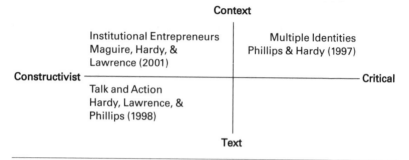

**Figure 4.1**    Our Approaches to Discourse Analysis

This contrasts with a second study (Hardy, Lawrence, & Phillips, 1998: Box 3.5 in Chapter 3), which examined how collaboration can be generated discursively. Here our interest was descriptive—how did collaboration come about—and the power relationships among participants were not a concern. Consequently, our first research question was much more general and focused simply on the processes of social construction: *How do the shared understandings, created by conversational activity (the workshop interactions) lead to collaborative action?* We were also interested in the microdynamics of discursive activity—in this case, the "text" we analyzed was the talk among participants in the collaboration workshop, rather than the broader context. There is then no mention of context in our research question. Instead, we try to gain a more finely grained understanding of the role of discursive activity in collaboration by focusing attention on three particular discursive constructions in our second research question: *How does conversational activity (the workshop interactions) generate collaboration by discursively producing identities, skills, and emotion?*

A third paper (Maguire, Hardy, & Lawrence, 2001; Box 3.3 in Chapter 3) examined how peripheral actors acted as institutional entrepreneurs and changed the institutional field in the Canadian HIV/AIDS treatment domain. In this case, context was crucial because of the unique nature of AIDS and the changes that had occurred, in terms of the emergence of a field of AIDS treatment and support organizations, since the advent of the disease. Here we focused on three research questions: *Who are the institutional entrepreneurs—are they to be found among peripheral actors in the field? What do they do—what activities comprise institutional entrepreneurship? What are the conditions of possibility—what characteristics of institutional fields make institutional entrepreneurship by peripheral actors more likely?* The research questions are descriptive—they are interested in the "who, what, and how" of institutional entrepreneurship—and have nothing explicitly to do with power. They do, however, direct attention toward the larger context in the form of the institutional field.

So far, we have not published a study that is critical and focuses on texts, although we are currently researching the role of texts in structuration processes, which is driven by an interest in using critical linguistic analysis to explore processes of change in the context of the Palestinian nongovernment organization (NGO) described in Box 3.4 in Chapter 3. This will allow us to explore the specific discursive activities of the manager, which enabled him to reconstitute the organization in a particular way and to examine the ensuing political effects. The fact that our work can be located in different parts of the framework reiterates the point made earlier: that as researchers conduct different projects to study different phenomena, they can and should explore different theoretical assumptions as a way to broaden their contribution to the field.

In summary, discourse analysis allows researchers to ask a variety of questions relating to the constructive effects of language—exploring the way in which the socially produced ideas and objects that constitute our "reality" are actually created and maintained. Within these broad parameters, researchers need to align their research questions with their relative interest in context versus text and in power versus description. Researchers interested in context need to construct research questions that draw them "outward," whereas those interested in texts need to ask questions that flesh out the microdynamics of their construction.

## Object of Study

The research question does not, however, depend solely on the research philosophy: The object under study is also critical. Discourse studies explore the discursive production of aspects of social reality. As a result, the phenomenon that is being studied, and how it is conceptualized, will influence the research question. Defining the object of study in terms of an existing literature and then framing a research question around it is a critical step in the design of a study. For example, much of our work has focused on identity, whereas another area of interest has been collaboration. Depending on the nature of the exact empirical object under study in a particular publication, different research questions drive the work, even within the context of the same broad research program. So, for example, our paper on whale watching (Lawrence et al., 1999a; Box 3.2 in Chapter 3) explores the discursive foundations of collaborative relationships. Accordingly, the three research questions explicitly relate to collaboration. The first is concerned with the conditions and resources that facilitate collaborative organizational behavior. The second concerns the nature of collaboration as a process, including the stages of collaboration, the politics, and the emotional aspects. The third asks about the results of collaboration. By understanding the discursive processes that connect the antecedents, dynamics, and outcomes of collaboration, we are in a better position to learn more about how collaboration can be managed and facilitated. In another study using the whale watching data (Lawrence & Phillips, 1997), our interest was in how macrocultural changes created the possibility of a new form of ecotourism. Specifically, our primary interest was the role played by the complex interdiscursive processes whereby whales as "monsters" or "natural resources" became transformed into whales as "friendly," "intelligent," "individuals" in facilitating the creation of a commercial whale-watching industry. Our research question was, naturally, quite different: *How does the macrocultural context influence the emergence of a new industry through the creation of identities?*

By carefully defining the object of study, discourse analysis can contribute new insights to existing streams of research on the particular phenomena. It requires careful thought on the part of researchers to think through how their study connects to other related studies and to form their research questions accordingly. In this way, the results of the research will be of greater interest to the broad community of scholars and not just to discourse theorists. Understanding this link provides the potential for discourse analysis to contribute to a wide range of substantive issues, as we have tried to do in our own work with regard to identity, collaboration, and trust.

## Theoretical Influences

It is not just the object of study that connects discourse studies to existing literatures; it is also the theoretical influences and traditions on which the researcher intends to draw. When designing a study, researchers always face the choice of whether to conduct more theoretically informed work or to let the data drive the research. Some discourse theorists challenge the very idea that we should connect studies of discourse to broader theoretical frameworks, arguing that we should instead allow the data to "speak for themselves" if we are to avoid academic and moral imperialism (Burman & Parker, 1993). In contrast, other researchers argue that studies in which theory "floats disconnected from any political position" raise problems of relativism (Burman & Parker, p. 167), making it difficult to evaluate situations and consider ways in which they might be changed (Parker, 2000).

Despite this debate, it is clear that discourse studies adopt both approaches regarding theory. Some researchers do focus primarily on data, letting it drive their work; others use particular theoretical traditions to influence research questions because they explicitly want to use discourse analysis to build on and complement existing theoretical developments. To the degree that studies are explicitly connected to particular bodies of work, this work should frame and shape the research question. This is a strategy that we have undertaken with our own work. For example, the research questions discussed earlier in the whale-watching study about the antecedents, dynamics, and outcomes of collaboration were intended to contribute to domain theory (e.g., Gray, 1989). The research questions on institutional entrepreneurship in Canadian HIV/AIDS treatment discussed above relate directly to institutional theory. In another paper using this data (Maguire, Phillips, & Hardy, 2001a), we developed research questions that relate to specific theories of trust and of control: *What are the dynamics of identification-based trust and normative control, and how can identification-based trust be generated?* In each case, the decision to connect with a particular body of theory led to an extended literature review out of which grew a relevant research question.

## Contribution

These issues—philosophy, object of analysis, and theory—are not unconnected. They interact and, taken together, help the researcher to ascertain the contributions that a particular study—and the use of discourse analysis—can make. We believe that this is a crucial consideration. If discourse analysis is to realize its potential and achieve a sustainable position within areas such as organization and management theory, organizational communication, and psychology, we need to be explicit about its contributions. These contributions can take a number of forms. They can extend existing understandings of a substantive area of research. In this way, we have sought to add to the understanding of areas such as identity, collaboration, strategy making, and trust. They can build on other theoretical perspectives.

Our own work has broadened its theoretical focus from critical discourse analysis to include domain theory, institutional theory, microsociology, and narrative theory. Finally, it is possible for empirical studies to contribute to the philosophical development of a broader field. More usually, it is the theoretical work on discourse that achieves this, and a number of writers have used discourse theory to comment on developments in disciplines such as organization and management theory (e.g., Alvesson & Kärreman, 2000a, 2000b; Chia, 2000), organizational communication (see Putnam & Fairhurst, 2001; Putnam, Phillips, & Chapman, 1996) and psychology (Harré, 1995; Parker, 1992; Potter, 1996; Potter & Wetherell, 1987). It is, however, also possible to use empirical studies to comment on theoretical developments in a field of study as, for example, Knights and Morgan's (1991) work on strategy has shown. In our own work, we have used our research on refugees as data to show how the academic community discursively constructs research subjects (Hardy et al., 2001).

By asking themselves a series of questions (see Box 4.1), researchers will be able to develop the research questions that will form the basis of their research. The research questions are also helpful in explaining the study to colleagues and research subjects, and provide a starting point for writing it up. We have found that well-constructed research questions provide a strong foundation for the rest of the study.

We do not deny that good studies can be carried out without an explicit research question, and certainly not all of our work has been designed in such a planned way, as we discuss later in the chapter. Over time, however, we have learned that stating research questions explicitly early on in the design of a study has been one of the most effective tools for designing, conducting, and publishing a research project using discourse analysis.

## Selecting a Site

The choice of a research site is generally based on two sets of considerations: theoretical concerns related to the research questions and more practical concerns about access and timing. Designing research questions beforehand can be useful in guiding the subsequent choice of site. Although we would certainly recommend this approach as an effective way to proceed, especially in the case of inexperienced researchers, such a linear process is a luxury not always available to researchers. We have on several occasions been presented with an interesting, opportunistic research site for which we

---

**Box 4.1**
**Research Questions**

- What research philosophy underpins your research?
- What is your object of study?
- Upon which theoretical influences are you drawing?
- What contribution do you hope to make?
- What is your research question?

---

have had to generate research questions. And, even when one begins with research questions, unforeseen problems—or opportunities—can require a change of plan. Fascinating research insights can still be gained from serendipitous access, and, to capitalize on them, researchers need to be receptive to all eventualities and able to juggle both theoretical and practical constraints in selecting a research site should the need arise.

## Theoretical Considerations

From a theoretical point of view, research sites should be "transparent" in the sense that they make the subject of inquiry easily visible (Eisenhardt, 1989). Eisenhardt advocated the use of "extreme" cases in which the theoretical implications are likely to be more visible (also see Dutton & Dukerich 1991). In our critical studies, it has meant selecting sites where there was obvious discursive struggle so that discursive activity was clearly evident and likely to be linked to ways in which individual actors sought to protect their interests. The choice of refugee systems as an arena in which to study discursive activity was logical given the obvious clash between discourses of humanitarianism and of sovereignty—the one driving for greater access for refugees and the other stipulating greater control of borders. This broader discursive struggle also clearly manifested itself in a struggle around refugee identity—whether as a deserving political refugee, bogus asylum seeker, or economic migrant. This struggle was readily apparent—a quick read of the newspapers and early exploratory work was all that was necessary to convince us that discursive struggle was pervasive. It was also clear that different groups had different stakes in the struggle, making the political and strategic issues in which we were interested easy to witness and document.

In this way, we have found a theoretical sampling approach useful, in which research sites are chosen based on the likelihood that they will provide theoretically relevant results (Glaser & Strauss, 1967; Yin, 1984). Because discourse studies are oriented toward theory creation rather than theory testing, choosing a site with particular characteristics, which make it more likely to produce certain differences or similarities that can be related to particular theoretical positions, is sensible. We have also used theoretical sampling to conduct multiple case studies. For example, we chose to study discursive aspects of the refugee systems in Canada, the United Kingdom, and Denmark because we knew that the three countries were very different on a number of important dimensions. For example, Canada's immigration policy allowed for large numbers of immigrants and refugees, and the country had been recognized for its "humanitarian" approach to asylum seekers by bodies such as the United Nations. The United Kingdom, on the other hand, had a far more restrictive immigration policy and was introducing a series of policies with the explicit intent of discouraging asylum seekers. Compared with these other two countries, Denmark had the most programmed approach to asylum seekers, housing them in reception centers when they arrived and offering a settlement program to those who were successful in securing refugee status. In addition, Canada was based on a federal system, compared with the more centralized systems in the other two counties. In other words, key characteristics of the refugee systems in the three countries made it likely that, by comparing and contrasting them, we could expect contrary results that could be explained with reference to discourse theory.

## Practical Considerations

In addition to these more theoretical concerns, practical considerations also shape the choice of a research site. Very simple considerations such as geographic proximity and language makes certain sites that might be theoretically interesting impractical. (On the other hand, they should not rule out research at a location which, while not necessarily the most convenient, nonetheless is likely to prove fruitful; we have conducted research in locations ranging from Denmark to Vancouver Island to Palestine and in settings that span ecotourism, the pharmaceutical industry, and refugee determination.) Conversely, research sites may present themselves unexpectedly, and access to an unusual setting cannot be easily dismissed. In fact, practicality can and should drive the choice of the research question if interesting sites present themselves and offer opportunities for insightful empirical research. When this situation occurs, as we discussed above, researchers must reverse the process and ask, What kind of research questions would be interesting to study in this context? This sort of opportunistic research can provide findings that are just as important and significant as more planned research.

Having a good understanding of the potential contributions of discourse analysis and the factors that underpin the choice of research design can help to make researchers more aware of opportunities as they present themselves. One example of opportunistic research related to our study of editorial cartoons on immigration (Hardy & Phillips, 1999). We acquired the cartoons as a result of conducting research on refugees—Canadian immigration authorities kept a collection of cartoons related to immigration and refugees during a particularly interesting period in Canada when the immigration legislation was changed. This gave us the idea of collecting all cartoons in Canadian newspapers during the same period, and we conducted a search to check our collection and fill any gaps. Having collected the data, we were convinced that it would be interesting and useful to study, although it took some time to come up with a sensible research question that could be used to frame a paper. We finally did so by asking, *How were the discursive strategies of individual actors in the refugee system [identified in an earlier paper] influenced by the broader context of relevant discourses that operate at a societal level?* The cartoons proved to be a way to tap into the broader discourse of immigration; they provided clues to and fragments of this wider discourse. In this case, then, we had collected the data before we developed the research question, but our belief in the value of the data helped us find an interesting research question that built on our earlier work.

Another aspect of opportunism concerns unexpected events that throw systems into chaos and reveal discursive moves that might otherwise be taken for granted and hidden. In this regard, we have, more than once, framed our studies around a "moment of crisis" to make visible "aspects of practices that might normally be neglected or normalized" (Woodilla, 1998, p. 41). Although researchers sometimes secure access to moments of crisis on a retroactive basis, some crises occur while the researcher is in the field. In this case, the challenge for the researcher is to recognize them and act on them. For example, in the case of our study of Mère et Enfant, we had originally selected the case as a result of our interest in interorganizational collaboration (Box 3.4 in Chapter 3). Shortly before conducting our interviews, however, the manager told us of the intervention of the security forces and explained his—discursive—response. We quickly became aware that he had a very real crisis on his hands and that we had an exciting research opportunity. These events added up to a relatively brief period during which the organization visibly changed from being an international NGO to a local one and then back to an international one as a result of discursive rather than material changes. In addition, the texts written and disseminated in conjunction with the change were readily available. We consequently amended the research design to collect the necessary additional data.

Another obvious opportunity for site selection is consulting. For example, our paper on the discursive basis of collaboration among employment service organizations (Box 3.5) came about when one of the coauthors, who had just been hired in a consulting role with the organizations, read an early version of a conference paper that we had written. The paper explicated a model that resonated with his early experiences, which we then "tested" by arranging for a research assistant to conduct interviews to complement our coauthor's participant observation role as consultant.

In some cases, then, the selection of a research site is less planned, and the systematic approach to developing a research question and using it to select a research site is reversed. Instead, researchers need to be able to intuit the potential of a research site and derive research questions and modify data collection appropriately to suit the circumstances.

In summary, good research in general, and discursive studies in particular, represent a balance of the planned and the emergent. The fact that we have been engaged in research *programs* means our approach varies. In some cases, we have started in a more planned way and then reacted to emergent research opportunities. In others, we have done the reverse. The key for researchers is to ask themselves the questions featured in Box 4.2 and to be aware of the research potential of the particular site.

## Collecting Data

The collection and management of data is particularly problematic for discourse analysts (Putnam & Fairhurst, 2001). Although it goes without saying that site selection in the case of discourse analysis depends on ready access to texts broadly defined, deciding on which texts to use as data is not simple. We define texts to include talk, written texts, nonverbal interactions, films, television programs, and other media, symbols, and artifacts.[1] One important question concerns which of the various sources of material constitutes data in the case of discourse analysis? Generally, "naturally occurring" texts—in the sense that they appear in the normal day-to-day

---

**Box 4.2**
**Selecting a Site**

- Does the research site have particular characteristics that make it likely to produce interesting results?
- Are research sites sufficiently similar or different along theoretical dimensions for comparative analysis?
- Is the research site likely to produce "transparent" findings?
- Has a good source of discursive data presented itself?
- Has a crisis occurred that will reveal insight into discursive activity?

---

activities of the research subjects—are considered a better source of data for discourse analysis because they are actual examples of language in use. By this we mean that the text forms part of the discourses that constitute the phenomenon under investigation. Which texts occur "naturally" in any particular situation depends on the research question, however.

For example, if the research question concerns the discursive construction of an organization, naturally occurring texts might include the different kinds of archival data that organizations store, such as e-mails, memos, internal reports, minutes of meetings, annual reports, as well as texts that accumulate outside the firm such as media articles, government reports, advertisements, and so forth. In addition, conversations and meetings among members of the organization and presentations by organizational members to outsiders, such as sales meetings, annual general meetings, presentations to customers, and board meetings, also represent talk that helps constitute the organization. In this case, researchers may need to videotape conversations and meetings, rather than rely on reports, so that they can apply their analysis to the "raw" text rather than someone's synthesis of it. Defining text even more broadly, one might make use of symbols (company logos, letterhead) and artifacts (buildings, furniture), as well as locations, facilities, and so forth. Clues to the discourse that constructs the organization can be found in all these different "texts" and in how they are produced, disseminated, and consumed. The researcher's aim is to engage in some form of systematic analysis of some subset of this wide variety of texts.

In this case, research interviews would not be classified as naturally occurring data but, rather, as researcher-instigated discourse. In other words, research interviews, of themselves, are not part of the discourse that constructs the organization. Although the talk of respondents in research interviews will bear some relation to the talk that they use to construct the organization, it is difficult to say exactly how much, and certainly the researchers' interests will have some bearing on the talk, regardless of how open-ended the interview is. As a result, some researchers eschew the use of interviews as data in discourse analytic studies. In contrast, we believe that interviews play a useful role in discourse analysis. At the very least, they are important for understanding the social context of the primary texts. For example, Hirsch (1986) used interviews with executives as a way to understand the evolution in the way corporate takeovers were perceived. We have used them to understand the complex interorganizational domains in which our discursive studies have taken place. In addition, given the practical constraints on research, they can provide a legitimate source of data, especially if complemented with other texts. They need to be interpreted with care, however, and researchers should realize that other forms of texts provide more direct insight into the relevant processes of social construction.

The important point of this discussion is that the texts that best constitute data depend on what the researcher is studying. If it is an organizational topic of inquiry, texts that are naturally produced in that context offer advantages over interviews. If the study is about the individual, then interviews may be less problematic because the way in which individuals construct themselves in an interview with a researcher may be similar to how they construct themselves in other arenas of talk. So, for example, Potter and Wetherell (1987) used talk in interviews as naturally occurring texts because they were interested in how individuals constructed themselves and others with reference to race. If researchers are interested in broader societal level discourses, then they will likely have to consult texts that are disseminated widely. We have, for example, used editorial cartoons to study immigration discourse, and films and novels to study changes in the social constructions of a whale.

Another problem facing researchers is choosing between texts. Given the myriad ways in which an organization is constructed, the challenge is not to find texts but deciding *which* texts to choose (and to justify that choice to reviewers). The difficulty for discourse analysts, then, is how to identify a manageable, relatively limited corpus of texts that is helpful in exploring the construction of the object of analysis. Box 4.3 explores these issues.

**Box 4.3**
**Data Collection at Citigroup**

In 1999, Citigroup was in the middle of an identity crisis. The cultures of the two companies that merged to form Citigroup were profoundly different, and little progress had been made in bridging the gap. It was clearly an interesting research site for anyone interested in identity and culture. One of the authors and a colleague approached the company and proposed a study, to which Citigroup agreed. In their proposal, the researchers had asked for permission to interview key Citigroup employees and to collect archival data that would reflect the countervailing discourses around the new identity. The company agreed that they could interview whomever they wished and that any documents they wished to consult would be made available. But, asked the company contacts, "What exactly do you want us to give you?" The new company had more than 160,000 employees scattered around the world in myriad offices. "Where would you like to collect your data?" "Who would you like to interview?" "What materials do you want?"

These questions were crucial ones that would determine the value of the study: What, exactly, would constitute data? How would the researchers sample the literally billions of available documents to produce a meaningful and manageable corpus of texts?

In the end, the decision was to focus on texts with the most impact—communications of various kinds from the head office to the entire company that were purposefully designed to influence the company's culture. These texts, combined with interviews of executives and a small number of randomly sampled employees, provided more than enough data.

*Note:* This research was carried out by Nelson Phillips and Steve Maguire, Faculty of Management, McGill University, Canada.

What is clear is that some form of sampling is essential—the question of what and how much to sample depends largely on the object of study, but researchers can try to capture "important" texts, for example, those that are widely distributed, that are associated with changes in practices, or that were produced in reaction to a particular event. They can consider texts that can be easily compared, for example, comparing two films about the same subject, comparing company logos, or comparing annual reports over time or from different organizations. They can also consider how to put "natural" limits around data collection, such as a particular time period.

In summary, discourses are not neatly packaged in a particular text or even in a particular cluster of texts. Researchers can only trace clues to them regardless of how much data they collect. Similarly, the interpretive nature of the analysis means that the researcher does not seek to exhaust categories, but to *generate* them by way of identifying how people use language. Consequently, the notion of saturation in discourse analysis is "elastic." The endpoint comes not because the researcher stops finding anything new, but because the researcher judges that the data are sufficient to make and justify an interesting argument (Wood & Kroger, 2000). The answers to the questions that the researcher must ask (Box 4.4) are, then, inherently subjective, but that does not mean they cannot be explained and justified.

## Analyzing the Data

Even when a researcher has decided which texts to select, the often-Herculean task of analyzing them still remains. The standardized methods that exist in more quantitative approaches are not appropriate for discourse analysis. Although freedom from such constraints provides considerable room for creativity, it does make the task of analysis somewhat daunting. It also means that discourse analyses regularly face criticism concerning a lack of "rigor." To be too systematic, too mechanical, undermines the very basis of discourse analysis, however, inducing the reification of concepts and objects that it seeks to avoid (Burman & Parker, 1993). The aim of discourse analysis is to identify (some of) the multiple meanings assigned to texts, which means that more systematic, laborsaving forms of analysis (such as traditional content analysis) are counterproductive because they aim at rapid consolidation of categories.

"Recipes" for successful data analysis are therefore difficult to provide. The breadth of discourse analysis techniques—from an emphasis on specific utterances to an analysis of a range of texts over time—and the diversity of the phenomena under investigation mean that the form that analysis takes will vary from study to study. As a result, researchers need to develop an approach that makes sense in light of their particular study and establish a set of arguments to justify the particular approach they adopt. Although

---

**Box 4.4**
**Collecting Data**

- What texts are most important in constructing the object of analysis?
- What texts are produced by the most powerful actors, transmitted through the most effective channels, and interpreted by the most recipients?
- Which of the above texts are available for analysis?
- Which of the above texts is it feasible to analyze?
- How will I sample these texts?
- How will I explain the choices I have made?

---

this individualist approach to analysis undoubtedly causes difficulties, particularly in convincing journal editors of the legitimacy of the analysis, it is in its contextual and interpretive sensitivities that the benefits of discourse analysis lie.

> Doing analysis is also like writing a paper in that although we sometimes follow the order of the final paper—writing the introduction, then the body, then the conclusion—we may also start in the middle, and regardless of where we begin, we expect that we return to and revise that section after we have written the others. . . . And as in writing a paper it is not always easy to decide when to stop and go with what you have. (Wood & Kroger, 2000, p. 97)

Given the emergent aspect of data analysis, it is impossible to provide a simple template for proceeding. Instead, we work through an example from our research to highlight the challenges.[2] As we mentioned earlier, in our study of immigration and refugee cartoons (Hardy & Phillips, 1999), we possessed a collection of editorial cartoons—a data set—awaiting a research question. We read and reread the cartoons and knew that if we could develop a structured approach to analyze them, they would provide us with insight into refugee systems. We realized that the cartoons were not just about refugees, but also about immigration more generally. As we worked through the cartoons and discussed what we were seeing, a research question slowly began to emerge. We had already identified discursive strategies of individual actors in an earlier paper, and our theoretical thinking emphasized that such discursive activity was inevitably influenced by broader discourses that operated at a societal level. We read a series of studies that had used cartoons as data in other contexts and found that they were regularly used as an indicator of macroconcepts. We decided that it was legitimate to use the cartoons as a fragment of broader immigration discourse. Given our view that discourse constructs objects and concepts, it became clear that we needed to (a) establish what the cartoons constructed and (b) examine how the constructions related to the individual strategies of actors in the refugee system.

We started by examining the cartoons to see which objects were represented in them. It was clear that refugees were represented, but so, too, was the government and the immigration system and, in some cases, the public. We went through all the cartoons together and identified which objects were represented in them. This first stage of the analysis showed us that different cartoons constructed these objects differently: In some cases, for example, refugees were constructed as frauds; in others, they were represented as victims. Similarly, in some cases, the government was depicted as cruel, in others as incompetent. So as a second step, we recoded all the cartoons in terms of the way in which they constructed the four objects. This was an iterative and collaborative (and time-consuming) process. We started by taking a few obvious examples and talking them through with each other—debating and discussing the various themes so that we had similar understandings of them and wrote up a definition of each theme (see Table 4.1). We then coded half the cartoons separately. We each then took the other through our coding, either "signing off" where we agreed or discussing cases where there was a disagreement until we did agree. By the end of this second stage of analysis, we were able to show that the cartoons constituted one or more of the four objects according to one or more of 17 themes.

Following this analysis, we were able to surmise how immigration discourse, as indicated by the cartoons, produces not only refugees, but also other objects such as the government, the immigration system, and the public. By seeing the different ways in which these objects were constructed, we were also able to consider how broader societal discourses provided resources to governments (e.g., refugees as frauds and the public as in need of protection necessitated the determination system) and NGOs (e.g., refugees as victims and the government as cruel, corrupt, and incompetent justified NGO protection). As far as refugee organizations were concerned, however, there were no such resources (due to the absence of any

**Table 4.1** Summary of Coding

| Actor(s) represented in the cartoon | Theme | Definition of theme |
|---|---|---|
| Refugee | Fraud | Those presenting themselves as refugees are in no danger |
| | Victim and fraud | Those presenting themselves as refugees may be either victim or fraud |
| | Victim | Those presenting themselves as refugees are at risk from persecution and warrant protection |
| | Privileged | Those presenting themselves as refugees gain quicker access to Canada than other immigrants |
| Government | Cruel | The government is unwilling to take responsibility for refugees |
| | Corrupt | Individuals in the government allow entry to Canada based on personal reasons |
| | Incompetent | The government is unable to administer the system effectively |
| | Under tension | The government is subject to contradictory and unresolvable tensions regarding its responsibility to refugees and the public |
| Immigration system | Inconsistent | Certain groups, such as illegal immigrants, fraudulent refugees, or individuals with political connections, are treated preferentially |
| | Inadequate | The determination system is unable to prevent large numbers of refugees from entering Canada |
| | Too tough | The determination system keeps out people who should be allowed in to Canada |
| | Too lenient | The determination system lets people in who should be kept out of Canada |
| | Too slow | The determination system takes too long to render decisions |
| | Gullible | Officials are unable to distinguish between genuine and fraudulent refugees |
| | Honorable | The determination system carries out its responsibilities toward refugees |
| Public | Requiring protection | The public requires protection from large numbers of refugees entering Canada |
| | Opposed | The public is opposed to refugees entering Canada |

representations of refugees as empowered, autonomous, or self-sufficient members of society).

There are several qualitative data analysis packages that researchers may find helpful in conducting discourse analysis (see Miles & Huberman, 1994, and Richards & Richards, 1991, for more information on such packages). Data such as transcripts and written documents are the most amenable to computer-assisted analysis, although some packages can be used to code visual data, such as cartoons and videos. These packages allow researchers to attach codes to particular pieces of text and then to perform various database functions on the coded text. When a researcher is working with large amounts of data, these packages provide a convenient and powerful tool for automating the repetitive and time-consuming administrative aspects of data analysis. It is, however, important to keep in mind that in the case of discourse analysis, the software is simply a way of automating and managing the subjective process of manual coding. It allows researchers to work through more data, but it does not "improve" the analysis in terms of the way in which the researcher explores multiple meanings and traces their implications—an inherently subjective process—and it certainly does not make the analysis any more "rigorous" or "valid." We have used software packages on some occasions and have undertaken analysis manually on others, mainly depending on the amount of data we have been trying to manage.

This is just one example of how we have approached data analysis, and it is designed to convey our experience rather than to provide a template—different researchers will use different methods depending on their studies. Some help can be obtained by other work in the area. So, for example, researchers interested in the micro aspects of individual conversations might consult Potter and Wetherell (1987) and Wood and Kroger (2000); those interested in macro texts can read Knights and Morgan (1991) or Fairclough (1992); those trying to make sense of different genres of text can examine Yates and Orlikowski (1992) and Orlikowski and Yates (1994). Even with the help of our example, the researcher will need to "customize" his or her method of analysis by answering the questions in Box 4.5.

## Writing Up the Study

Like other forms of qualitative research, discourse analytic studies are as much about writing as they are about data collection or data analysis. And just as there is a need to be creative in developing workable

---

**Box 4.5**
**Data Analysis**

- How will I analyze my data?
- What sort of data do I have, micro or macro?
- What sort of categories do the data generate?
- Do these categories relate to my research question?
- Can I explain and justify my choice of categories?
- How will I know when to stop?

---

approaches to data analysis, there is also a need to develop innovative—and convincing—ways of presenting data, methods, and results. Currently, there are few established norms or standards specifying how to write up a study in terms of what to include and how to justify theoretical conclusions. The limited number of published studies provides some guidance, but many intractable problems remain. At the most basic level, discourse analysis is not institutionalized, so researchers face the ongoing struggle of convincing reviewers and editors that their studies are conducted satisfactorily and that their papers written appropriately. In addition, discourse analytic studies do not fit well within the conventional length restrictions of an academic paper. Researchers face the continual problem of trying to fit too much material into too little space. Explaining the research question, the research site, the method of data collection and analysis, and the findings generally requires more space than is available. The fact that there are few conventions for data collection and data analysis means that a convincing narrative must be developed to explain to readers what was done and why. Researchers who have answered the questions posed in this chapter will, however, find themselves relatively well placed to construct an effective narrative (Box 4.6).

In constructing this narrative, the aim is to ensure that readers, especially editors and reviewers, understand why and how the findings are legitimate. In this regard, the researcher has to construct arguments that are very different from work undertaken under the auspices of other epistemologies. Issues of validity and reliability do not play out in the same way. Validity—the idea that the research closely captures the "real" world—is not relevant when epistemological and ontological assumptions maintain that there is no

---

**Box 4.6**
**Constructing a Persuasive Narrative**

---

- What is the research question?
- Why did I choose the research site?
- What data did I collect and why?
- How did I analyze the data?
- How does the analysis address the research questions?
- What contributions does this research make?

---

"real" world other than one constructed through discourse. Reliability—the idea that the results are "repeatable"—is nonsensical when one is interested in generating and exploring multiple—and different—readings of a situation (Wood & Kroger, 2000). This does not mean that readers cannot (and will not) make judgements about the value of a piece of work. How well the evidence is presented to demonstrate the arguments, how plausible the findings are, and how profound the analytic scheme is in helping readers to make sense of discourse can and will all be evaluated (Wood & Kroger, 2000). In addition, reviewers will be looking for how sensitive researchers are to the different ways in which language constructs phenomena, the degree to which they offer interesting and insightful interpretations, the ability with which they incorporate historical and contextual understandings, and the extent to which they are aware of the political nature of empirical material (Alvesson & Deetz, 2000; also see Weick, 1999; Whetten, 1989).

## Make It Interesting

As we said at the beginning of this chapter, the nature of discourse analysis makes designing and conducting a discourse analytic study more art than science. Coming up with an interesting research question, finding a site, collecting data, analyzing it, and writing it up requires creativity and innovation for every new study. As a result, discourse analysis is a difficult process, which can be almost as difficult the tenth time as the first. While we are unable to provide a standard method for researchers to follow, we can provide some general guidelines. We can also point readers to the increasing number of resources available to assist them in developing their studies. More empirical studies are appearing in the literature to provide exemplars of good discourse analytic research. More books (including this one) are discussing discourse analysis as a method. More conferences and workshops are being organized for researchers active in this area. These resources provide a very useful reservoir of ideas and approaches from which researchers can draw in designing new studies.

But there is one thing we haven't really mentioned, which is absolutely crucial to the success of any study: Whatever you do, the results must be *interesting* to someone. Simply being well constructed and well conducted does not mean that a study will be published. What makes a study publishable is that it contributes to the literature which, in turn, means that there must be an audience to find it relevant and interesting. This raises an important question: What makes a study interesting? According to Davis (1971), it must do one of three things. It must show that something we thought was one thing is actually another; that two things we thought were different are actually the same; or that two things we thought were the same are different. In other words, what is interesting depends on showing a group of researchers something that surprises them which, of course, depends on the commonly accepted thinking of the time and which is, therefore, highly contextual. Nevertheless, researchers must have an idea of who their audience is. These points can be summarized in the final and most important questions that researchers need to ask themselves: What makes this study interesting? and To whom will it be interesting?

## Notes

1. See Wood and Kroger (2000, p. 68) for examples of the many sources of discourse data.
2. This summary appears in Hardy (2001).

## 5. CONCLUSIONS

We wrote this book because we believe discourse analysis has the potential to contribute significantly to our understanding of social phenomena. Our enthusiasm grows out of several sources. It grows out of the experience of actually doing discourse analytic studies and being happily surprised at the results. It grows out of reading the work of others and finding it insightful, interesting, and valuable. And it grows out of observing the direction and development of social science and seeing more opportunities for discourse analytic methods to contribute a much needed new perspective on important areas of inquiry. At the same time, we recognize that there are significant challenges facing researchers who are using discourse analysis in their work. In particular, there are problems of making a distinct contribution, of keeping discourse analysis focused on discourse, and of developing solutions to some of the methodological problems that plague discourse analysis. Although we believe that the potential of discourse analysis far outweighs the challenges, both deserve our attention here. In this conclusion, we therefore focus on the contributions and challenges of discourse analysis.

## Contributions

The most important contribution of discourse analysis is that it provides a way to unpack the production of social reality. Although the linguistic turn has led to a growing acceptance of a social constructivist epistemology, traditional qualitative methods provide more insight into the meaning of social reality than into its production. Discourse analysis provides a sympathetic epistemology and a set of methods which are useful for empirically exploring social construction. Introducing the idea of a discourse, in addition to text and context, provides the critical dimension that allows social construction to be understood. It is not individual texts that produce social reality, but structured *bodies* of texts of various kinds—discourses—that constitute social phenomena. By examining the nature of a discourse, including the methods of textual production, dissemination, and reception that surround it, we can understand how the concepts that make social reality meaningful are created. Discourse analysis therefore provides the tools to investigate a whole set of processes that underlie individual, organizational, and interorganizational phenomena.

Using organization and management theory as an example, this can be put simply: Discourse analysis provides the tools to understand the social processes that produce organizations. This contribution is even more important when we consider that many of the more recent topics that have been the focus of intense research activity, such as the knowledge-based firm, the virtual organization, globalization, and e-commerce, strain existing theoretical frames. We require new approaches if we are to understand the dynamics of these new phenomena. In addition, new theoretical ideas such as poststructuralist conceptualizations of identity and cognition also demand new approaches to their investigation.

But there is also a second, more subtle contribution: Discourse analysis pushes researchers to think carefully about their own research practices. The linguistic turn in organizational and management theory has led to calls for increased reflexivity on the part of researchers (Clegg & Hardy, 1996a; Hardy et al., 2001; Linstead, 1994), which means paying attention to "the interpretive, political and rhetorical nature of empirical research" (Alvesson & Sköldberg, 2000, p. vii). Reflexivity involves reflecting on the ways in which research is carried out and understanding how the process of doing research shapes its outcomes (Holland, 1999). It acknowledges that all references to empirical data are the results of interpretation—there are no unmediated data—and incorporates an understanding of how the researcher, research community, and society collectively play a role in the social construction of "knowledge" (Alvesson & Sköldberg, 2000; Hardy et al., 2001; Kaghan & Phillips, 1998). "Researchers interrogate their own world as well as that of their subjects and generate new insights by investigating interruptions. Their research is neither self nor subject oriented but is concerned with the dialectics of the relationship" (Linstead, 1994, p. 1327).

Writers have identified a number of characteristics or dimensions of research that deserve attention (e.g., Alvesson & Sköldberg, 2000; Hardy & Clegg, 1997; Jermier 1985; Linstead, 1994). First, researchers must take care to remember that language constructs, rather than reveals, reality—this applies not just to the language used by the subjects of research, but also to the language that is used to write up the research project. Second, researchers should ground their research in historical processes to understand how things come to be the way they are and how this history delimits the possibilities for action. Third, researchers should allow different voices to pervade the text, with particular consideration of voices that are normally silenced. They should explicitly consider the processes and implications of inclusion and exclusion for the way in which "reality" is experienced. Fourth, at the same time researchers need to acknowledge that they cannot include all potential voices: Although it is possible to identify some actors that might be missed by more traditional research, researchers—even discourse analysts—cannot stand outside the discourses in which they are located, and some actors and subject positions will remain invisible. Moreover, researchers cannot express the different voices that they do identify on equal terms. Some voices will be privileged over others by the way in which the research is conducted and written up and by the way in which (and degree to which) the researcher inserts him or herself into the text. Fifth, as a result, researchers must remember that theirs is but one representation and, rather than try to fortify it and close out alternate representations, they should open it up to multiple meanings and readings. Sixth, research should avoid totalizing theory and, instead, engage in debate among and between theoretical communities because it is difficult to critique a theory (and a representation) on its own terms. We need different points of reference if we are to interrogate our own work. Seventh, in writing up and presenting their work, researchers should not hide behind dominant conventions of text production and engage, unthinkingly, in the rhetoric that helps them to produce knowledge. Rather, we need to take full responsibility for our role in producing our own research texts. Finally, we should be aware of the political aspects of research and acknowledge that we construct knowledge through the research process. In this way, we come full circle and acknowledge that, as users of language, we use it to construct what passes for knowledge.

Much of the work that advocates reflexivity is theoretical in nature and eschews methodological discussion, downplaying empirical research altogether (Alvesson & Sköldberg, 2000; Clegg & Hardy, 1996a; Weick, 1999). But if we are to achieve reflexivity in a field of study, we cannot simply confine it to theorizing—we must be able to carry out empirical research according to its strictures. We believe that discourse analysis helps researchers to do exactly that: It involves an epistemology sympathetic to the postmodern ideas that underlie the linguistic turn and, at the same time, provides a method that helps researchers apply these ideas to an empirical setting. In Table 5.1, we summarize dimensions of reflexivity and show how discourse analysis can help researchers to enact those dimensions in their empirical work.

Combined, these two contributions highlight one of the characteristics of discourse analysis that we find the most interesting and important: its subversive nature.[1] Discourse analysis subverts and challenges taken-for-granted understandings and undermines the tendency to reify and solidify knowledge. From a discourse perspective, all versions of social reality are social constructions held in place by ongoing processes of discursive production. There are no "true" representations of reality from which one can critique other, somehow less real, versions. Although some versions are more legitimate and held in place by more powerful processes, they are all equally products of human interaction and subject to the same dynamics.

**Table 5.1** Reflexivity and Discourse Analysis

| Dimension of reflexivity | Role of discourse analysis |
| --- | --- |
| Acknowledge that language constructs rather than reveals. | Discourse analysis rests on a basic assumption that language constructs social "reality" rather than acting as a route to the discovery of an objective reality. |
| Ground research in historical processes. | Discourse analysis is inherently processual in nature: We can only understand particular texts by understanding how they interact with broader discourses and other texts. |
| Allow different voices to pervade the text. | Discourse analysis is particularly interested in locating voices that are normally missed through more traditional research methods; by applying discourse analysis to research sites that are transparent, in crisis, or beset with struggle, we can uncover previously silenced voices. |
| Acknowledge that not all possible voices appear in the text, and those that do are not expressed on equal terms. | Discourse analysis is based on the premise that a discourse can never be studied in its entirety, merely that clues to it can be found in texts, of which only a small subset of texts can be identified, collected, and analyzed, reinforcing awareness of the incomplete nature of the research project, and the inevitable absence of some voices. In addition, critical discourse approaches that focus on how subjects are positioned differently by discourse provide a way to explore the positioning of subjects within an academic text. |
| Engender multiple meanings and alternate representations. | Discourse analysis is fundamentally interpretive, and discourse analytic techniques aim explicitly at uncovering multiple meanings and representations. |
| Engage in debate among and between theoretical communities. | Discourse analysis is not characterized by a unified, convergent theory, making theoretical totalization less of a risk; by using discourse analysis to inform and complement other bodies of theory, we can stimulate debate. |
| Take responsibility for our texts. | The lack of institutionalized techniques and rituals in discourse analysis makes it difficult to hide behind dominant conventions and rhetoric; instead, authors often have to "customize" their analysis and carefully explain their work. |
| Be aware of political aspects of research. | As discourse analysis is applied to empirical studies and the process of research, the political feature of the research process and our own writing becomes more apparent. |

Furthermore, all versions of reality can be analyzed using the techniques of discourse analysis to explore the processes of social construction and the role of interested actors. This includes the more traditional topics of interest to social scientists, new topics that are just appearing, and social science itself. Discourse analysis destabilizes and undermines taken-for-granted notions and provides a much-needed way to throw into sharp relief the web of discourses that supports the social reality that research subjects and researchers alike encounter in their everyday lives.

## Challenges

Although we are confident and excited about the future of discourse analysis, we also see major challenges ahead. The first and most important challenge we face is to develop the necessary methods to make discourse analysis truly discursive. Currently, there are far too many papers with contributions reduced by a failure to adequately consider the discursive level in their analysis. The three-level conception of text, discourse, and context is too often reduced to a two-dimensional analysis that only links text and context while failing to explore the role of the discourses of which the text is a part. There is nothing wrong per se with the notion of connecting texts to contexts. Approaches such as semiotics, hermeneutics, and narrative analysis have long looked for the constructive effects of texts by looking at the text–context relationship. The unique contribution of discourse analysis, however, is to insert the discursive level to understand how structured sets of text and the practices of their production, dissemination, and reception together constitute the social. No aspect of social reality depends on a single text, or even on all the texts that exist in a particular setting. Instead, texts belong to discourses—structured collections of texts—and are made meaningful by the numerous other texts on which they draw intertextually, the complex relations between texts, and the particular elements of the socially constructed world in which they are produced. The aim of discourse analysis is to study these bodies of texts that constitute discourse. Although dealing with this discursive level is immensely difficult, it is critical to the contribution of discourse analysis and therefore to its future.

The second challenge we face is that discourse analysts must begin to carve out a niche in which their unique contribution is recognized. It is not enough to point over and over again to the potential of discourse without being specific as to what this potential comprises. It is also important to contribute to other substantive bodies of literature. Unless we are able to engage with and build on existing, ongoing streams of literature, we will be doomed to increasing marginalization. In many ways, the work of Michel Foucault has suffered this fate. Although his work was initially met with tremendous enthusiasm, the difficulties of applying his particular form of discourse analysis were so significant that researchers were generally unable to apply it in a way that contributed to the broader literature. As a result, it has become a perspective that, many people agree, is interesting but that has been unable to sustain the theoretical potential and promise it was once considered to offer.

A third challenge is that a number of difficult practical problems with data collection and analysis remain and require better solutions than currently exist. Many of these challenges were mentioned in Chapter 4, and we will not repeat ourselves here. Nonetheless, much work remains to develop more "standardized" solutions to the basic problems of discourse analysis in an organizational context. As these solutions are identified and become institutionalized, it will become easier to conduct studies, to write up the results, and to get research published. Practically, this offers considerable advantages for researchers. At the same time, however, researchers must avoid the disadvantages of standardization and institutionalization—with shared norms, there often comes unthinking research rituals that can lead researchers to conduct and write up their work uncritically and unreflexively.

## On a Personal Note

Returning for a moment to the beginning of this book, Rushdie's character recognized that it was a particular discourse that made him what he was. It is this observation—that it is discourse that constitutes the social—that continues to excite us. Discourse analysis is challenging and risky, but it provides important insight into the most basic questions about the constitution of the social world. Rather than limiting ourselves to the study of reified "things," we can begin to unravel the mysteries of social construction that produce societies, organizations, and individuals. For us, this is a tremendously exciting project, and we hope that this book conveys our excitement. We also hope that it has provided some help to others interested in making a contribution to the general program of research that is growing out of discourse analysis. Although there are challenges, we hope we have made a convincing case for the potential benefits. We also hope that many of the

88

readers of this book will join us in exploring the ways in which discourse analysis can help us understand "the diverse warring descriptions of ourselves" (Rushdie, 2000, p. 510).

## Note

1. We would like to thank Tom Keenoy for this important observation.

## REFERENCES

Ainsworth, S. (2001, June). 'The feminine advantage': A discursive analysis of the invisibility of older women workers. Paper presented at Rethinking Gender Work and Organization Conference, Keele University, Keele, England.

Alvesson, M., & Deetz, S. (1996). Critical theory and postmodern approaches in organizational studies. In S. R. Clegg, C. Hardy, & W. R. Nord (Eds.), Handbook of organization studies (pp. 191–217). London: Sage.

Alvesson, M., & Deetz, S. (2000). Doing critical management research. London: Sage.

Alvesson, M., & Kärreman, D. (2000a). Taking the linguistic turn in organizational research: Challenges, responses, consequences. Journal of Applied Behavioral Science, 36, 136–158.

Alvesson, M., & Kärreman, D. (2000b). Varieties of discourse: On the study of organizations through discourse analysis. Human Relations, 53, 1125–1149.

Alvesson, M., & Sköldberg, K. (2000). Reflexive methodology: New vistas for qualitative research. London: Sage.

Alvesson, M., & Willmott, H. (1992a). On the idea of emancipation in management and organization studies. Academy of Management Review, 17, 432–464.

Alvesson, M., & Willmott, H. (Eds.). (1992b). Critical management studies. London: Sage.

Anderson-Gough, F., Grey, C., & Robson, K. (2000). In the name of the client: The service ethic in two professional services firms. Human Relations, 53, 1151–1174.

Beech, N. (2000). Narrative styles of managers and workers: A tale of star-crossed lovers. Journal of Applied Behavioral Science, 53, 210–218.

Benton, T. (1981). Objective interests and the sociology of power. Sociology, 15, 161–184.

Berger, P. L., & Luckmann, T. (1967). The social construction of reality: A treatise on the sociology of knowledge. Garden City, NY: Anchor.

Boje, D. M. (1995). Stories of the storytelling organization: A postmodern analysis of Disney as "Tamara-Land." Academy of Management Journal, 38, 997–1035.

Bourdieu, P. (1993). Sociology in question. London: Sage.

Braverman, H. (1974). *Labor and monopoly capital.* New York: Monthly Review Press.

Burawoy, M. (1979). *Manufacturing consent.* Chicago: University of Chicago Press.

Burman, E., & Parker, I. (1993). Against discursive imperialism, empiricism and constructionism: Thirty-two problems with discourse analysis. In E. Burman & I. Parker (Eds.), *Discourse analytic research: Repertoires and readings of texts in action* (pp. 155–172). London: Routledge.

Burrell, G. (1988). Modernism, postmodernism and organizational analysis: The contribution of Michel Foucault. *Organization Studies, 9,* 221–235.

Calás, M. B., & Smircich, L. (1991). Using the "F" word: Feminist theories and the social consequences of organizational research. In A. Mills & P. Tancred (Eds.), *Gendering organizational analysis* (pp. 222–234). London: Sage.

Chalaby, J. K. (1996). Beyond the prison-house of language: Discourse as a sociological concept. *British Journal of Sociology, 47,* 684–698.

Chia, R. (2000). Discourse analysis as organizational analysis. *Organization, 7,* 513–518.

Clegg, S. R. (1975). *Power, rule, and domination.* London: Routledge.

Clegg, S. R. (1987). The language of power and the power of language. *Organization Studies, 8,* 61–70.

Clegg, S. R. (1989). *Frameworks of power.* London: Sage.

Clegg, S. R., & Hardy, C. (1996a). Representations. In S. R. Clegg, C. Hardy, & W. R. Nord (Eds.), *Handbook of organization studies* (pp. 676–708). London: Sage.

Clegg, S. R., & Hardy, C. (1996b). Introduction. In S. R. Clegg, C. Hardy, & W. R. Nord (Eds.), *Handbook of organization studies* (pp. 1–29). London: Sage.

Cobb, S., & Rifkin, J. (1991). Neutrality as a discursive practice: The construction and transformation of narratives in community mediation. *Studies in Law, Politics, and Society, 11,* 69–91.

Collins, R. (1981). On the microfoundations of macrosociology. *American Journal of Sociology, 86,* 984–1013.

Condor, S., & Antaki, C. (1997). Social cognition and discourse. In T. A. van Dijk (Ed.), *Discourse as structure and process: Volume 2* (pp. 676–708). London: Sage.

Cooper, R., & Burrell, G. (1988). Modernism, postmodernism and organizational analysis: An introduction. *Organization Studies, 9,* 91–112.

Coulon, A. (1995). *Ethnomethodology.* Thousand Oaks, CA: Sage.

Covaleski, M. A., Dirsmith, M. W., Heian, J. B., & Sajay, S. (1998). The calculated and the avowed: Techniques of discipline and struggles over identity in the Big Six public accounting firms. *Administrative Science Quarterly, 43,* 293–327.

Czarniawska, B. (1998). *A narrative approach to organization studies.* Thousand Oaks, CA: Sage.

Davis, M. (1971). That's interesting! Toward a phenomenology of sociology and a sociology of phenomenology. *Philosophy of Social Science, 1,* 309–344.

De Cock, C. (1998). It seems to fill my head with ideas: A few thoughts on postmodernism, TQM, and BPR. *Journal of Management Inquiry, 7,* 144–153.

Denzin, N. K., & Lincoln, Y. S. (1994). *Handbook of qualitative research.* London: Sage.

DiMaggio, P. J., & Powell, W. W. (1983). The iron cage revisited: Institutional isomorphism and collective rationality in institutional fields. *American Sociological Review, 48,* 147–160.

Dirlik, A. (1999). Globalization and the politics of place. In K. Olds, P. Dicken, P. F. Kelly, L. Knong, & H. Wai-Chung Yeung (Eds.), *Globalization and the Asia-Pacific: Contested territories* (pp. 39–56). London: Routledge.

du Gay, P. (1996). *Consumption and identity at work.* London: Sage.

Dunford, R., & Jones, D. (2000). Narrative in strategic change. *Human Relations, 53,* 1207–1226.

Dutton, J. E., & Dukerich, J. M. (1991). Keeping an eye on the mirror: Image and identity in organizational adaptation. *Academy of Management Journal, 34,* 517–554.

Edwards, R. (1979). *Contested terrain.* New York: Basic Books.

Eisenhardt, K. M. (1989). Building theories from case study research. *Academy of Management Review, 14,* 532–550.

Ellingson, S. (1995). Understanding the dialectic of discourse and collective action: Public debate and rioting in antebellum Cincinnati. *American Journal of Sociology, 101,* 100–144.

Erickson, K., & Stull, D. (1997). *Doing team ethnography.* Thousand Oaks, CA: Sage.

Fairclough, N. (1992). *Discourse and social change.* Cambridge, UK: Polity Press.

Fairclough, N. (1995). *Critical discourse analysis: The critical study of language.* London: Longman.

Fairclough, N., & Wodak, R. (1997). Critical discourse analysis. In T. A. van Dijk (Ed.), *Discourse as social interaction: Volume 1* (pp. 258–284). Sage: London.

Fineman, S. (1996). Emotion and organizing. In S. R. Clegg, C. Hardy, & W. R. Nord (Eds.), *Handbook of organization studies* (pp. 543–564). London: Sage.

Fletcher, J. K. (1998). Relational practice. A feminist reconstruction of work. *Journal of Management Inquiry, 7,* 163–186.

Foucault, M. (1965). *Madness and civilization: A history of insanity in the age of reason.* New York: Vintage.

Foucault, M. (1972). *The archeology of knowledge.* London: Routledge.

Fournier, V., & Grey, C. (2000). At the critical moment: Conditions and prospects for critical management studies. *Human Relations, 53,* 7–32.

Gamson, J. (1995). Must identity movements self-destruct? A queer dilemma. *Social Problems, 42,* 390–408.

Garnsey, E., & Rees, B. (1996). Discourse and enactment: Gender inequality in text and context. *Human Relations, 49,* 1041–1064.

Geertz, C. (1973). *The interpretation of cultures.* New York: Basic Books.

Gergen, K. (1991). *The saturated self.* Newbury Park, CA: Sage.

Gergen, K. (1999). *An invitation to social construction.* London: Sage.

Gill, R. (1993a). Justifying injustice: Broadcasters account of inequality in radio. In I. Parker & E. Burman (Eds.), *Discourse analytic research* (pp. 75–93). London: Routledge.

Gill, R. (1993b). Ideology, gender, and popular radio: A discourse analytic approach. *Innovation, 6,* 323–339.

Glaser, B., & Strauss, A. (1967). *The discovery of grounded theory: Strategies for qualitative research.* Chicago: Aldine.

Grant, D., Keenoy, T., & Oswick, C. (1998). Organizational discourse: Of diversity, dichotomy and multi-disciplinarity. In D. Grant, T. Keenoy, & C. Oswick (Eds.), *Discourse and organization* (pp. 1–14). London: Sage.

Gray, B. (1989). *Collaborating: Finding common ground for multiparty problems.* San Francisco: Jossey–Bass.

Hardy, C. (1985). The nature of unobtrusive power. *Journal of Management Studies, 22,* 384–399.

Hardy, C. (1994). Understanding interorganizational domains: The case of refugee systems. *Journal of Applied Behavioral Science, 30,* 278–296.

Hardy, C. (2001). Researching organizational discourse. *International Studies in Management and Organization, 31*(3), 25–47.

Hardy, C., & Clegg, S. R. (1996). Some dare call it power. In S. R. Clegg, C. Hardy, & W. R. Nord (Eds.), *Handbook of organization studies* (pp. 622–641). London: Sage.

Hardy, C., & Clegg, S. R. (1997). Relativity without relativism: Reflexivity in post-paradigm organization studies. *British Journal of Management, 8,* S5–S17 [special issue].

Hardy, C., Lawrence, T., & Phillips, N. (1998b). Talking action: Conversations, narrative, and action in interorganizational collaboration. In D. Grant, T. Keenoy, & C. Oswick (Eds.), *Discourse and organization* (pp. 65–83). London: Sage.

Hardy, C., Palmer, I., & Phillips, N. (2000). Discourse as a strategic resource. *Human Relations, 53*(9), 7–28.

Hardy, C., & Phillips, N. (1998). Strategies of engagement: Lessons from the critical examination of collaboration and conflict in an interorganizational domain. *Organization Science, 9,* 217–230.

Hardy, C., & Phillips, N. (1999). No joking matter: Discursive struggle in the Canadian refugee system. *Organization Studies, 20,* 1–24.

Hardy, C., Phillips, N., & Clegg, S. R. (2001). Reflexivity in organization and management studies: A study of the production of the research "subject." *Human Relations, 54,* 3–32.

Hardy, C., Phillips, N., & Lawrence, T. B. (1998). Distinguishing trust and power in interorganizational relations: Forms and façades of trust. In C. Lane & R. Bachmann (Eds.), *Trust within and between organizations* (pp. 64–87). Oxford, UK: Oxford University Press.

Harré, R. (1995). Discursive psychology. In J. A. Smith, R. Harré, & L. van Langenhove (Eds.), *Rethinking psychology* (pp. 143–159). Thousand Oaks, CA: Sage.

92

Heracleous, L., & Barrett, M. (2001). Organizational change as discourse: Communicative actions and deep structures in the context of information technology implementation. *Academy of Management Journal, 44,* 755–778.

Hirsch, P. M. (1986). From ambushes to golden parachutes: Corporate takeovers as an instance of cultural framing and institutional integration. *American Journal of Sociology, 91,* 800–837.

Holland, R. (1999). Reflexivity. *Human Relations, 52,* 463–485.

Holmer-Nadeson, M. (1996). Organizational identity and space of action. *Organization Studies, 17,* 49–81.

Holmes, J. (1998). Women's talk: the question of sociolinguistic universals. In J. Coates (Ed.), *Language and gender: A reader* (pp. 461–483). Oxford, UK: Blackwell.

Hoskins, K., & Maeve, R. (1987). The genesis of accountability: The West Point connections. *Accounting, Organizations and Society, 12,* 37–73.

Jackall, R. (1988). *Moral mazes: The world of corporate managers.* New York: Oxford University Press.

Jackson, B. G. (2000). A fantasy theme analysis of Peter Senge's *Learning Organization. Journal of Applied Behavioural Science, 36,* 193–209.

Jermier, J. (1985). When the sleeper wakes: A short story extending themes in radical organization theory. *Journal of Management, 11*(2), 67–80.

Kaghan, W. N., & Phillips, N. (1998). Building the Tower of Babel: Communities of practice and paradigmatic pluralism in organization. *Organization, 5,* 191–217.

Keenoy, T., Oswick, C., & Grant, D. (1997). Organizational discourses: Text and context. *Organization, 2,* 147–158.

Kleiner, B. (1998). The modern racist ideology and its reproduction in "pseudoargument." *Discourse and Society, 9,* 187–215.

Knights, D., & Morgan, G. (1991). Corporate strategy, organizations, and subjectivity: A critique. *Organisation Studies, 12,* 251–273.

Kress, G. (1995). The social production of language: History and structures of domination. In P. Fries & M. Gregory (Eds.), *Discourse in society: Systemic functional perspectives* (pp. 169–191). Norwood, NJ: Ablex.

Langellier, K. M., & Peterson, E. E. (1993). Family storytelling as a strategy of social control. In D. Mumby (Ed.), *Narrative and social control: Critical perspectives* (pp. 49–76). Newbury Park, CA: Sage.

Laumann, E. O., & Knoke, D. (1987). *The organizational state.* Madison: University of Wisconsin Press.

Lawrence, T., & Hardy, C. (1999). Building bridges for refugees: Toward a typology of bridging organizations. *Journal of Applied Behavioral Science, 35,* 48–70.

Lawrence, T., & Phillips, N. (1997, May). *From* Moby Dick *to* Free Willy: *The discursive construction of a cultural industry.* Paper presented at the conference on Research Perspectives on the Management of Cultural Industries, Stern School of Management, New York University, New York.

Lawrence, T., Phillips, N., & Hardy, C. (1999a). Watching whale watching: A relational theory of organizational collaboration. *Journal of Applied Behavioral Science, 35,* 479–502.

Lawrence, T., Phillips, N., & Hardy, C. (1999b). A relational theory of organizational collaboration. In S. Clegg, E. Ibarra, & L. Bueno (Eds.), *Global management: Universal theories and local realities* (pp. 246–264). London: Sage.

Lewicki, R. J., & Bunker, B. B. (1995). Trust in relationships: A model of development and decline. In B. B. Bunker, J. Z. Rubin, & Associates (Eds.), *Conflict, cooperation and justice: Essays inspired by the work of Morton Deutsch* (pp. 133–173). San Francisco: Jossey–Bass.

Linstead, S. (1994). Objectivity, reflexivity, and fiction: Humanity, inhumanity, and the science of the social. *Human Relations, 47,* 1321–1345.

Lukes, S. (1974). *Power: A radical view.* London: Macmillan.

Lutz, C. A., & Collins, J. L. (1993). *Reading* National Geographic. Chicago: University of Chicago Press.

Macnaghten, P. (1993). Discourses of nature: Argumentation and power. In I. Parker & E. Burman (Eds.), *Discourse analytic research* (pp. 52–72). London: Routledge.

Maguire, S., Phillips, N., & Hardy, C. (2001a). When "Silence = Death" keep talking: Trust, control and the discursive construction of identity in the Canadian HIV/AIDS treatment domain. *Organization Studies, 22,* 287–312.

Maguire, S., Hardy, C., & Lawrence, T. (2001b). *Peripheral actors as institutional entrepreneurs in the elaboration of institutional fields: HIV/AIDS treatment advocacy in Canada.* Paper presented at the conference of the European Group on Organization Studies, Lyons, France.

Maile, S. (1995). The gendered nature of managerial discourse: The case of a local authority. *Gender, Work and Organization, 2,* 76–87.

Marcus, G. E. (1994). What comes (just) after "post"? The case of ethnography. In N. K. Denzin & Y. S. Lincoln (Eds.), *Handbook of qualitative research* (pp. 563–574). London: Sage.

Mauws, M. K. (2000). But is it art? Decision making and discursive resources in the field of cultural production. *Journal of Applied Behavioral Science, 36,* 229–244.

McCann, J. E. (1983). Design guidelines for social problem-solving interventions. *Journal of Applied Behavioral Science, 19,* 177–189.

Miles, M., & Huberman, A. (1994). *Qualitative data analysis* (2nd ed.). Thousand Oaks, CA: Sage.

Morgan, G., & Sturdy, A. (2000). *Beyond organizational change: Structure, discourse, and power in UK financial services.* London: Macmillan.

Mumby, D. (1992). Two discourses on communication, power, and the subject: Jürgen Habermas and Michel Foucault. In G. Levine (Ed.), *Construction of the self* (pp. 81–104). New Brunswick, NJ: Rutgers University Press.

Mumby, D. K. (Ed.). (1993). Narrative and social control: Critical perspectives. Newbury Park, CA: Sage.

94

Mumby, D. (2000). Power and politics. In F. Jablin & L. L. Putnam (Eds.), *The new handbook of organizational communication* (pp. 585–623). Thousand Oaks, CA: Sage.

Mumby, D., & Putnam, L. L. (1992). The politics of emotion: A feminist reading of bounded rationality. *Academy of Management Review, 17,* 465–486.

Mumby, D., & Stohl, C. (1991). Power and discourse in organization studies: Absence and the dialectic of control. *Discourse and Society, 2,* 313–322.

Nkomo, S., & Cox, T. (1996). Diverse identities in organizations. In S. R. Clegg, C. Hardy, & W. R. Nord (Eds.), *Handbook of organization studies* (pp. 338–356). London: Sage.

O'Connor, E. S. (1995). Paradoxes of participation: Textual analysis and organizational change. *Organization Studies, 16,* 769–803.

O'Connor, E. S. (2000). Plotting the organization: The embedded narrative as a construct for studying change. *Journal of Applied Behavioral Science, 36,* 174–192.

Orlikoswki, W. J., & Yates, J. (1994). Genre reporting: The structuring of communicative practices in organizations. *Administrative Science Quarterly, 39,* 541–574.

Orr, J. E. (1996). *Talking about machines: An ethnography of a modern job.* Ithaca, NY: Cornell University Press.

Parker, I. (1992). *Discourse dynamics.* London: Routledge.

Parker, I., & Burman, E. (1993). Against discursive imperialism, empiricism and constructionism: Thirty-two problems with discourse analysis. In E. Burnam & I. Parker (Eds.), *Discourse analytic research* (pp. 155–172). London: Routledge.

Parker, M. (2000). The less important sideshow: The limits of epistemology in organizational analysis. *Organization, 7,* 519–523.

Phillips, N., & Brown, J. (1993). Analyzing communication in and around organizations: A critical hermeneutic approach. *Academy of Management Journal, 36,* 1547–1576.

Phillips, N., & Hardy, C. (1997). Managing multiple identities: Discourse, legitimacy and resources in the UK refugee system. *Organization, 4,* 159–186.

Phillips, N., Lawrence, T., & Hardy, C. (2000). Interorganizational collaboration and the dynamics of institutional fields. *Journal of Management Studies, 37,* 23–43.

Phillips, N., & Ravasi, D. (1998, July). *Analyzing social construction in organizations: Discourse analysis as a research method in organization and management theory.* Paper presented at the Third International Conference on Organizational Discourse: Pretexts, Subtexts and Contexts, London.

Potter, J. (1996). *Representing reality: Discourse, rhetoric, and social construction.* London: Sage.

Potter, J., & Wetherell, M. (1987). *Discourse and social psychology: Beyond attitudes and behaviour.* London: Sage.

Psathas, G. (1995). *Conversation analysis.* Thousand Oaks, CA: Sage.

Putnam, L. L., & Fairhurst, G. (2001). Discourse analysis in organizations: Issues and concerns. In F. M. Jablin & L. L. Putnam (Eds.), *The new handbook of organizational communication: Advances in theory, research, and methods* (pp. 235–268). Thousand Oaks, CA: Sage.

Putnam, L. L., Phillips, N., & Chapman, P. (1996). Communication in organizations. In S. R. Clegg, C. Hardy, & W. R. Nord (Eds.), *Handbook of organization studies* (pp. 375–408). London: Sage.

Richards, L., & Richards, T. J. (1991). The transformation of qualitative method: Computational paradigms and research processes. In N. Fielding & R. Lee (Eds.), *Using computers in qualitative research* (pp. 38–53). Newbury Park, CA: Sage.

Riessman, C. K. (1993). *Narrative analysis*. Newbury Park, CA: Sage.

Riggins, S. H. (1997). The rhetoric of othering. In S. H. Riggins (Ed.), *The language and politics of exclusion* (pp. 1–30). Thousand Oaks, CA: Sage.

Rosenau, P. M. (1992). *Post-modernism and the social sciences: Insights, inroads, and intrusions*. Princeton, NJ: Princeton University Press.

Rushdie, S. (2000). *The ground beneath her feet*. New York: Picador.

Salzer-Mörling, M. (1998). As God created the earth: A saga that makes sense? In D. Grant, T. Keenoy, & C. Oswick (Eds.), *Discourse and organization* (pp. 104–118). London: Sage.

Schegloff, E. A. (1992). In another context. In A. Duranti & C. Goodwin (Eds.), *Rethinking context* (pp. 191–228). Cambridge, UK: Cambridge University Press.

Schwartzman, H. (1993). *Ethnography in organizations*. Newbury Park, CA: Sage.

Shapiro, D. L., Sheppard, B. H., & Cheraskin, L. (1992). Business on a handshake. *Negotiation Journal, 8,* 365–377.

Sherzer, J. (1987). A discourse-centred approach to language and culture. *American Anthropologist, 89,* 295–309.

Sillince, J. A. (1999). The role of political language: Forms and language coherence in the organizational change process. *Organization Studies, 20,* 485–518.

Smircich, L. (1983). Concepts of culture and organizational analysis. *Administrative Science Quarterly, 28,* 339–358.

Spicer, A. (2000). *Discourses of globalisation: A theoretical framework*. Department of Management working paper, University of Melbourne, Australia.

Stokoe, E. H. (1998). Talking about gender: The conversational construction of gender categories in academic discourse. *Discourse and Society, 9,* 217–240.

Tannen, D. (1994). *Gender and discourse*. Oxford, UK: Oxford University Press.

Tolbert, P. S., & Zucker, L. G. (1996). Institutionalization of institutional theory. In S. R. Clegg, C. Hardy, & W. R. Nord (Eds.), *Handbook of organization studies* (pp. 175–190). London: Sage.

Townley, B. (1993). Foucault, power/knowledge and its relevance for human resource management. *Academy Management Review, 18,* 518–545.

van Dijk, T. A. (1993). Principles of critical discourse analysis. *Discourse and Society, 8,* 5–6.

van Dijk, T. A. (1996). Discourse, power and access. In C. R. Caldas-Coulthard & M. Coulthard (Eds.), *Texts and practices* (pp. 84–104). London: Routledge.

van Dijk, T. A. (1997a). *Discourse as structure and process: Volume 1*. London: Sage.

van Dijk, T. A. (1997b). *Discourse as social interaction: Volume 2*. London: Sage.

Warren, R., Rose, S., & Bergunder, A. (1974). *The structure of urban reform*. Lexington, MA: DC Heath.

96

Watson, T. J., & Bargiela-Chiappina, F. (1998). Managerial sensemaking and occupational identities in Britain and Italy: The role of management magazines in the process of discursive construction. *Journal of Management Studies, 35,* 285–301.

Weick, K. (1999). Theory construction as disciplined reflexology: Tradeoffs in the 90s. *Academy of Management Review, 24,* 797–806.

Weiss, R. M., & Miller, L. E. (1987). The concept of ideology in organizational analysis: The sociology of knowledge or the social psychology of beliefs. *Academy Management Review, 12,* 104–116.

Welcomer, S. A., Gioia, D. A., & Kilduff, M. (2000). Resisting the discourse of modernity: Rationality versus emotion in a hazardous waste site. *Human Relations, 53,* 1175–1206.

Wetherell, M. (2001). Debates in discourse research. In M. Wetherell, S. Taylor, & S. J. Yates (Eds.), *Discourse theory and practice: A reader* (pp. 380–399). Thousand Oaks, CA: Sage.

Wetherell, M., & Potter, J. (1992). *Mapping the language of racism: Discourse and the legitimation of exploitation.* New York: Harvester.

Whetten, D. (1989). What constitutes a theoretical contribution? *Academy of Management Review, 14,* 301–313.

Willmott, H. (1993). Strength is ignorance, slavery is freedom: Managing culture in modern organizations. *Journal of Management Studies, 30,* 515–552.

Wilson, F. (1996). Research note: Blind and deaf to gender? *Organization Studies, 17,* 825–842.

Winch, P. (1958). *The idea of a social science.* London: Routledge & Kegan Paul.

Witten, M. (1993). Narrative and the culture of obedience at the workplace. In D. Mumby (Ed.), *Narrative and social control: Critical perspectives* (pp. 97–118). Newbury Park, CA: Sage.

Wittgenstein, L. (1967). *Philosophical investigations.* Oxford, UK: Blackwell.

Wodak, R. (1991). Turning the tables: Anti-Semitic in post-war Austria. *Discourse and Society, 2,* 65–83.

Wodak, R. (1996). The genesis of racist discourse in Austria since 1989. In C. R. Caldas-Coulthard & M. Coulthard (Eds.), *Texts and practices: Readings in critical discourse analysis* (pp. 107–128). London: Routledge.

Wood, L. A., & Kroger, R. O. (2000). *Doing discourse analysis: Methods for studying action in talk and text.* Thousand Oaks, CA: Sage.

Woodilla, J. (1998). Workplace conversations: The text of organizing. In D. Grant, T. Keenoy, & C. Oswick (Eds.), *Discourse and organization* (pp. 31–50). London: Sage.

Yates, J., & Orlikowski, W. J. (1992). Genres of organizational communication: A structurational approach to studying communication and media. *Academy of Management Review, 17,* 299–326.

Yin, R. (1984). *Case study research: Design and methods.* Beverly Hills, CA: Sage.

Zbaracki M. K. (1998). The rhetoric and reality of Total Quality Management. *Administrative Science Quarterly, 43,* 602–636.

# ABOUT THE AUTHORS

**Nelson Phillips** is the Beckwith Professor of Management Studies at the Judge Institute of Management at the University of Cambridge. Before joining the Judge Institute, he was an Associate Professor in the Faculty of Management of McGill University. His research interests include discourse analysis, organizational collaboration, and a general interest in the intersection of cultural studies and organizational analysis. He has published a number of articles and book chapters, including articles in the *Academy of Management Journal, Journal of Management Studies, Journal of Management Inquiry, Business & Society, Journal of Business Ethics, Business Ethics Quarterly, Organization Science, Organization*, and *Organization Studies.*

**Cynthia Hardy** has been Professor of Management in the Department of Management, University of Melbourne, Australia, since 1998. Before 1998, she was a Professor in the Faculty of Management at McGill University in Canada. Her current research interests focus on organizational discourse theory and discourse analysis, and power and politics in organizations, especially with regard to interorganizational collaboration and strategy making. In total, she has published 12 books and edited volumes, including the *Handbook of Organization Studies*, published by Sage, which won the 1997 George R. Terry Book Award at the Academy of Management. She has written more than 60 journal articles and book chapters. Her work has appeared in many leading international journals, including the *Academy of Management Journal, Organization Studies, Journal of Management Studies, Human Relations, Organization Science, California Management Review,* and *Journal of Applied Behavioral Studies.*

# Qualitative Research Methods

## Series Editor
### JOHN VAN MAANEN
*Massachusetts Institute of Technology*

## Associate Editors:
**Peter K. Manning,** *Northeastern University*
**& Marc L. Miller,** *University of Washington*

**Other volumes in this series listed on outside back cover**